AF395564

THE WARRIOR WALKER

How I Found Resilience, Purpose and
Meaning on Britain's Coastline

PAUL HARRIS

First published in the UK in 2026 by Blink Publishing
An imprint of Bonnier Books UK
5th Floor, HYLO, 105 Bunhill Row,
London, EC1Y 8LZ

A CIP catalogue record for this book is available from the British Library.

Hardback ISBN: 9781785128691

Also available as an ebook and an audiobook

1 3 5 7 9 10 8 6 4 2

Design and Typeset by Envy Design Ltd
Printed and bound by CPI (UK) Ltd, Croydon CRO 4YY

The authorised representative in the EEA is Bonnier Books UK (Ireland) Limited.
Registered office address:
Block B, The Crescent Building
Northwood, Santry
Dublin 9, D09 C6X8
Ireland
compliance@bonnierbooks.ie

www.bonnierbooks.co.uk

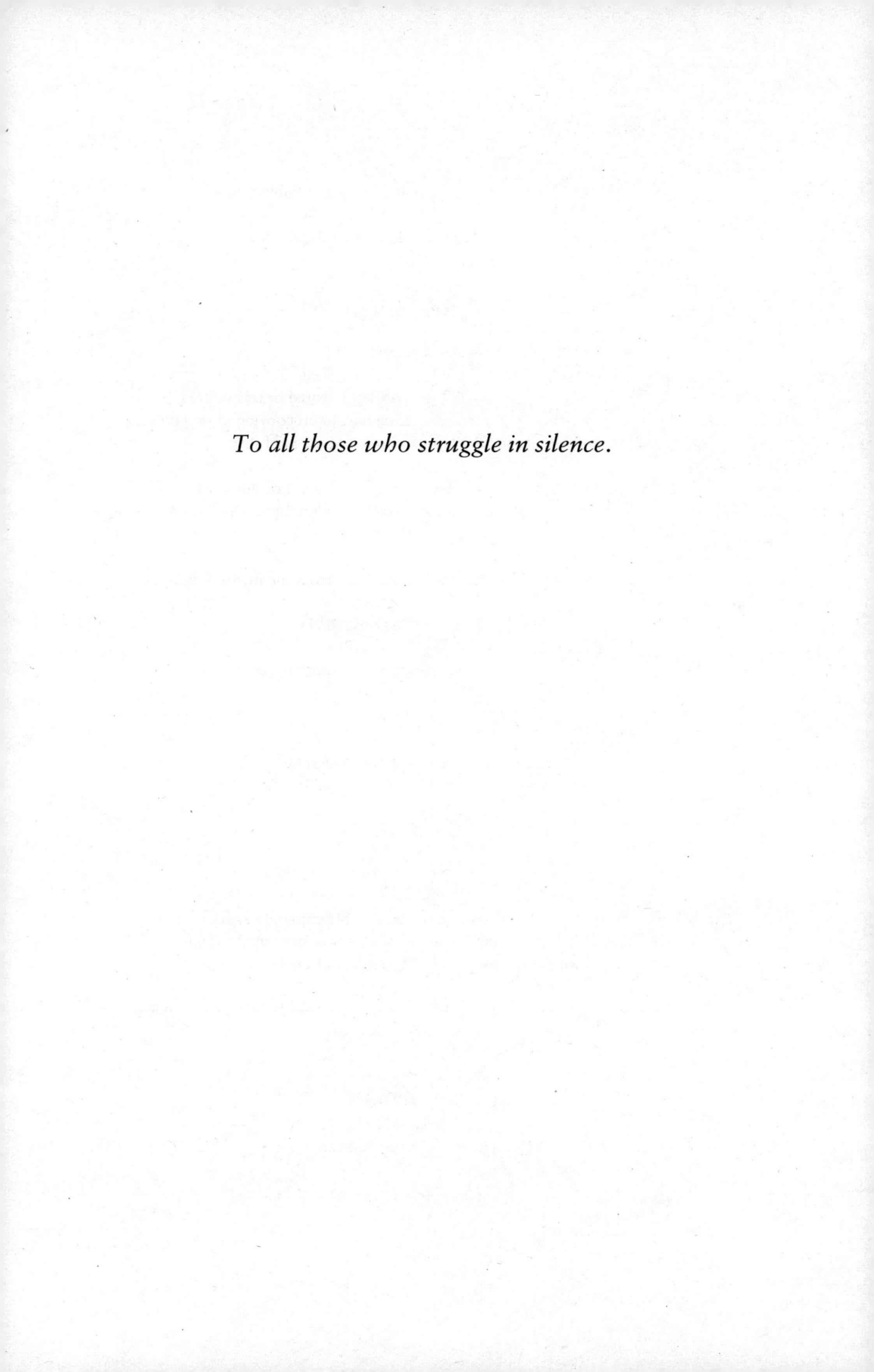

To all those who struggle in silence.

CONTENTS

Author's Note		ix
Chapter 1	**THE FIRST STEPS**	1
Chapter 2	**A BOX OF BROKEN BISCUITS**	5
Chapter 3	**I'M GONNA BE**	17
Chapter 4	**UNBURDENING**	27
Chapter 5	**BLOOD OF THE STONE**	39
Chapter 6	**THE ALMOST UNBEARABLE KINDNESS OF STRANGERS**	51
Chapter 7	**A POSTCARD FOR THE UNIVERSE**	59
Chapter 8	**FORGIVE, FORGET**	71
Chapter 9	**THE WHISPERINGS OF THE PATH**	83
Chapter 10	**REMEMBER YOU WILL DIE**	93
Chapter 11	**CHOICES**	103
Chapter 12	**A RESTING PLACE**	117

Chapter 13 **RIPPLES INTO WAVES** 129

Chapter 14 **A NORTHERN SOUL** 141

Chapter 15 **BATTLE-SCARRED** 155

Chapter 16 **ME VERSUS ME** 165

Chapter 17 **WHAT NEXT? (WHO CARES?)** 179

Chapter 18 **RED PILL/BLUE PILL** 189

Chapter 19 **A LITTLE HELP** 203

Chapter 20 **ALICE** 213

Chapter 21 **BOOK CLUB** 223

Chapter 22 **WHAT'S MEANT FOR YOU WON'T PASS YOU BY** 233

Chapter 23 **HUMANS CAN DO HARD THINGS** 243

Chapter 24 **YOU'LL NEVER WALK ALONE** 255

Chapter 25 **A STILLNESS** 267

Acknowledgements 277

AUTHOR'S NOTE

I never actually thought I would become an author but then, as you're about to read within these pages, I never thought I would do many things I have done in my life.

This journey and that first step taken back in July 2020 now seem like only yesterday but also many years ago.

The power of walking, human connection, the great outdoors and asking, 'Hey, how are you?' really has changed my life.

I hope you will enjoy what you will read within these pages and ultimately, I hope it makes you want to go for a walk and share your troubles with people.

The stories I will tell you are from my memory of my life and are my opinions from the path of my life.

Thank you for buying this book and I want to say a big thank you to all of you who helped me thus far in any way, shape or form – big or small. You know who you are.

It inspires me to do what I do to this day.
See you out on the path.

Paul

CHAPTER ONE

THE FIRST STEPS

LULWORTH COVE, JULY 2020

Ever stood at a bus stop or sat in a busy pub and experienced the unnerving sensation that someone is eyeballing you?

The feeling is usually intangible; it's a sixth sense thing, rather than a sign. But it's overwhelming and inescapable, as the skin shivers with goosebumps and the hairs prickle across the back of the neck. In Afghanistan, while going about my business with a private security firm, I often took these cues as a warning that something terrible was going to happen. In civilian life, though, it carried an altogether different vibe. That I'd probably drawn attention to myself for reasons that were either very good or very bad. Wild camping on a clifftop above the horseshoe-shaped coastline of Lulworth Cove in Dorset was an incongruous place for it to happen though. I was well hidden. There was a starlit sky around me, a claustrophobic silence smothered the landscape for miles and a gentle, summery breeze riffled across the sand and grass above my foxhole.

I looked around. *Nobody can see me out here, surely? Let alone stare . . .*

Then a large black mass blocked out a chunk of the Milky Way. My stomach tightened. A giant, man-sized shape loomed ominously and I feared my first night on the South West Coast Path – the opening steps in a Hail Mary journey that was supposed to bring some hope to a desperately hopeless chapter in my life – was about to end in violence. *What a terrible start.*

I'd never been homeless before, but now my entire life was stuffed into a Bergen backpack weighing around 30 kilos. But while I was equipped for all conditions, I was unaware of the rules of wild camping and that suddenly felt like a terrible oversight. If there was some unwritten code of conduct between the part-time travellers that walked the coastal trails for fun and the homeless and the desperate that were doing it out of necessity, then I had no idea of those rules and what they entailed. The former Royal Marine in me had chosen to make camp in a large natural divot in the ground. Having wrapped myself in a sleeping bag, I'd immediately fallen asleep, but this might have a been a major error. *What if I've inadvertently stepped into someone's territory?*

There was a surge of adrenaline as my eyes adjusted to the darkness and an instantly recognisable angular shape, all jagged edges and gnarled bone, edged closer.

Antlers. It was a bloody stag.

The thing was huge. A loud, explosive snort came from its nostrils and I felt its warm breath on my face. God, it stank!

Like wet dog and damp gym kit. Kicking away the sleeping bag in a panic, I scrambled to the lip of my foxhole and edged backwards, wondering whether anyone had ever been killed by one of the marauding beasts. In my former military life, I'd been taught how to stand up to the enemy, but I couldn't recall any instructions on what to do when confronted by an intimidating animal. All sorts of questions pinged around my brain. I knew there were different survival techniques to use when staring down a brown, black or grizzly bear – *should I use the same approach here?* I wasn't even sure if the bloody thing was passive, aggressive, or violently territorial, but not wanting to take any chances, I frantically pulled my kit together and jogged along the coastal path to a nearby church for shelter. A quick search on my phone revealed that stags were relatively harmless – but they were loaded with spiritual meaning. For native North American tribes, these proud animals were a symbol of strength, spiritualism and courage; of protection and the beginning of a new journey. Some people considered them to be indications of impending rejuvenation, transformation and enlightenment.

Telling myself that I'd overreacted and that everything was going to be fine, I slept fitfully on the church's doorstep, stirring every hour, on the hour, when the church bells clanged triumphantly. With each waking jolt, I cursed my plan and tested my resolve with a simple question:

Mate, what are you doing?

The honest answer was that I really didn't know.

CHAPTER TWO

A BOX OF BROKEN BISCUITS

The madcap idea to walk around Britain, unsupported, living out of the rucksack on my back, had landed at my feet a few weeks earlier. I'd been yomping from Bournemouth to Corfe Castle, a favourite walk of mine, as I tried to piece my life together. The views were amazing. Miles of sugar-sandy beaches swept into the distance. That June day was a chilly but calm one, and the molten yellow sun burned brightly above me. It seemed to pool in smouldering blobs across the water. From a patch of high ground, I was able to pick out Bournemouth and Poole. Ahead of me was Corfe Castle and the beautiful Dorset landscape. Trying to capture the moment, I recorded a short story for any Instagram mates that might have been scrolling by.

Like I was living my best life.

It's hard to say what was going on with me in that moment,

other than I was a right mess. Maybe the combination of fresh air and big skies had created an illusion of temporary freedom in a pandemic lockdown where everyone was being confined to their houses for months on end. In all that claustrophobia and misery, the sea sometimes offered a brief psychological escape. The endless slate waters calmed my anxiety. The crushing tightness in my chest ebbed away with the tide. And the vaguest hint of hope sometimes flickered on the horizon. All of it said: *Better days are coming.*

But when I turned inland, reminders of my broken life story dotted the landscape like tombstones. In the distance was the church where I'd been christened, in a village not too far away from where my adversarial dad lived. Over there was the area I'd grown up in: picture postcard villages that thrummed with tourists in the summer but, for the rest of the time, mainly felt like a lifetime of rainy Sundays. It was as much a part of me as I was of it, but rather than offering a sense of familial comfort and safety, it left me feeling exposed, naked, as if I'd been emotionally stripped down to nothing by a succession of heartbreaks and failures.

Like I was living my worst life.

Most days, I struggled to get out of bed. A breakdown seemed like one spilled coffee away. Before the first wave of lockdowns, I even went to see my GP because I was feeling so desolate. Sat in a sterile, soulless surgery, I struggled to articulate exactly what was happening to me, other than the fact that I seemed to be in a constant state of fight or flight. (Where flight seemed like the best option but I didn't have anywhere to run to.)

'I feel cornered in Bournemouth,' I'd blurted out.

It was a desperate attempt to diagnose my misery and it barely scratched the surface. The truth was that a turbulent family life had left some gnarly battle scars. Dad abandoned me and my brother when I was little, though he became more present during my thirties, which was something, I supposed. Our relationship was unsurprisingly moody. Meanwhile, Mum was hardly the most devoted of guardians and if it hadn't been for my grandparents, who often rescued us at weekends, I'd have likely fallen apart at the seams. Nan took me in, cheered me up and made me feel loved, becoming Mum and Dad and a best friend all in one. When both she and my grandad passed away during my thirties, I was devastated and took to wearing Nan's St Christopher locket, the patron saint of travellers, around my neck to keep her close. A photo of them was tucked inside my wallet, as a break-glass-in-case-of-emergency reminder of happier times. The scene: one moment from a holiday on the Isle of Skye in Scotland. They would go there often and I'd joined them on one trip when I was around 13. They are sitting together, smiling, on the ferry to Portree, the island's 'capital'. Grandad, dressed in a bright yellow cagoule and white t-shirt, still with a full head of brown hair, laughing. Nan, looking windswept, smiling kindly, her coat zipped up because she was cold, despite the woolly red rollneck she's wearing. They made me feel as if I was part of a proper family and my heart bruised every time I plucked the picture from its resting spot, somewhere between a couple of bank cards.

Despite their care and support, I suffered from a crushing shyness as a kid. At school, I rattled emotionally, like a box of broken custard creams. I wasn't very good at mixing with others; I had very few mates at school and if I did make friends, I barely spoke to them. My saving grace was sport. I represented the county at long-distance running and was good enough at football to have taken it very seriously, but I didn't because of my fear of showering in front of the other boys – another symptom of those crippling insecurity issues. Then, when my eighteenth birthday approached, Mum gave me an ultimatum: *Either join the military or I'm kicking you out.*

Oh, fuck, I thought.

Not long afterwards, I was down the road at the Commando Training Centre Royal Marines (CTCRM) in Lympstone, where I signed up for 32 weeks of basic training. I was about to become a bootneck. *Welcome to hell.*

I'd only joined the military to see if I could bloody do it but, having passed out of training, I served as a commando for four and a half years before leaving in 2007. At first, I felt unsure of what to do next. I took up a place at Cardiff University, where I intended to study sports coaching because that's what my then girlfriend was doing. But just as the course was about to start, I switched on the telly and watched a brand new reality TV show called *Shipwrecked,* a game in which two competing teams of athletic, single and horny 20-somethings competed for a cash prize on a remote tropical island, all while wearing very little clothing. When a request for new contestants flashed up on the screen, I waggled the remote control at the TV excitedly. I was going to apply, I decided.

'Go for it,' laughed my girlfriend. 'You'll never get on.'

But I did, and having lied about my relationship status on the application form, I was soon flying to the Cook Islands, where

I spent two months surrounded by a gang of very good-looking men and women, our every move filmed by TV cameras. The concept of acting naturally for an audience of millions didn't come as easily to me as it did some of the other contestants, nor did pretending to be single, and like a typical Marine, I kept my secrets close. For a brief while I even slept at the opposite end of the beach from the rest of the gang. Eventually, my walls came down and I joined in with a reality TV family in which everyone cared for one another and tight bonds were formed. Or so it seemed.

It was only once I'd returned home to England that life got weird. Repeats of *Shipwrecked* seemed to be playing every night and it became inescapable, a real water cooler TV event, in the vein of *Big Brother*. Worse was that on some episodes, I was the main character, especially on those evenings when I'd slept away from the group. There were national discussions as everyone tried to suss out the weird ex-Marine, and whether I was a total oddball. I can remember several painful episodes when the *Shipwrecked* cast – people I'd grown to like and trust – spoke about me behind my back. The comments were hurtful. And even though social media – which was mainly Myspace and Facebook – wasn't as toxic as it is today, I soon experienced a certain level of online attention and drama.

Some of it was fun though. 'Paul from Shipwrecked', or 'Paul "Marine" Harris', became a recognisable alter ego and there were lots of parties, lots of booze and, when my girlfriend later became an ex, lots of one night stands. But without a job I was soon flat broke and eventually used my military experience to land a gig as a contractor in Afghanistan, where

I provided personal security for local politicians, NGOs and foreign journalists operating in the Badlands. The work was fun but spicy, and we weren't given weapons licences, so as an understandable precaution, everybody armed themselves off the books. We were then told that if the local authorities discovered we were carrying AK-47s, everyone would be arrested. A compromise was made whereby we sometimes went out without weapons. *What could possibly go wrong?* I thought. My carefree naivety evaporated one afternoon when a bloke responsible for the company's payroll was robbed and beheaded by the Taliban outside the bank. Suddenly, the adventurous life felt a little heavy.

I wasn't in a good place emotionally and warning signs were flashing at me everywhere I looked. Whenever I took a holiday, I flew to Thailand and life there suited me just fine. It was hot and the people were kind; the beer was cheap and the pace of life was slow. But I was obviously frazzled. I hated the thought of going back to the blood and fear of Afghanistan, and I often woke up with a start in the middle of the night, my heart banging at the sound of a barking dog or a spluttering car engine. Deciding that the contractor's life was behind me, in 2014, I took up an English teacher's position in Bangkok, where I schooled Thai children between the ages of four and 12. At first, the gig was challenging and a lot more intimidating than anything I'd ever done before. While I'd been involved in a few skirmishes with the Taliban, nothing gave me the butterflies like a class of giggling infants as they tried to learn the lyrics to 'Ba Ba Black Sheep'. It was bloody terrifying.

In those days, the rules in Thailand regarding ex-pats and their employment visas were loose. A Brit or an American worker on a three-month ticket was required to leave the country for a few days. Then, having seen out some time in a neighbouring country, their 90-day limit was reset and the process started all over again. *Oh, happy days*, I thought. The authorities didn't seem to care and everyone involved was comfortable with the sketchy system. For a teacher like me, there was even money to be made. Whenever a colleague went away on what was called a visa run, I covered their shifts and scooped up the overtime – and they did the same for me. I was living the dream: making money, working hard in an exotic country and having loads of fun. I even had a serious girlfriend, Joy, who ran her own accounting and auditing firm.

Then everything changed.

Following a visa run in 2019, bureaucracy hit me like a ton of bricks. A desk clerk at the embassy looked at my passport. 'No,' he said, riffling through the pages. 'You've done this too many times.'

I felt the panic rising in my chest. *Too many times?* I'd never experienced any problems before. None of us had. 'What do you mean?'

'I mean, you'll have to go home, wait six months and then apply for another visa in London.' He pushed my passport back across the desk with a dead-eyed stare.

'There has to be another way?' I said, feeling panicked. My life was unravelling at a terrifying velocity.

The clerk smiled thinly. 'Yes, there is. But it involves a fee of £20,000.'

Twenty grand? I knew I'd been pulled into a scam but there was nothing I could do. (Even if the money could have bought me a new visa, I didn't have it.) My life in Thailand had been built up over seven years and I had roots. But within a week, I was singing 'Ba Ba Black Sheep' with the kids for the very last time and kissing Joy goodbye at the airport, wondering how our relationship could possibly be sustained on FaceTime and WhatsApp for half a year.

My days became a misery. Dad begrudgingly allowed me to move in with him in Bournemouth for a bit and I picked up work at a nearby insurance firm, where I pushed my pen around a desk all day, staring through the window at the pouring rain and the grey. It wasn't long before my relationship with Joy started to fray, and our conversations shortened and tightened with the distance. There were days when I sat at my workstation and sobbed. Nobody around me knew why or how to help. I'd gone from living my best life in Thailand to my worst and I wanted desperately to go back, but I couldn't. Because I'd been away from the UK so long, I didn't have many friends to call upon. My old insecurities came rushing back and I stopped talking to people at work because I didn't feel as if I could trust them. Then the self-talk turned toxic. I hated myself. Whenever I looked in the mirror, there was so much self-loathing I struggled to maintain eye contact.

The panic attacks started shortly afterwards. Christmas was approaching, my relationship with Joy was in its final, inevitable stages, and I was about to spend the holidays alone because nobody truly loved or cared for me. My grandparents were gone, I didn't have any long-term friends in the area and it wasn't like I got on very well with Dad either. This desolate mood became increasingly suffocating until one evening, my chest tightened painfully. I dropped to my knees and gasped for air, like a climber at extreme altitude.

Oh my god, am I about to die?

Unable to move or call anyone for help, I sobbed and choked for ten minutes. Then the crushing pressure around my heart and lungs melted away and I was able to draw down several deep gulps of air.

The first few words out of my mouth connected me to a worrying reality: *I feel like a failure.*

And then, chillingly: *I don't want to be here anymore.*

Going for a long walk along the nearby coastal path and clifftops seemed like the only way to avoid something terrible from happening – though subconsciously, I might have been looking for a suitable location to commit a final, fatalistic act. Fortunately, the very first stroll helped to clear my head, albeit temporarily. The same thing happened on the next walk and the next, and I realised that, even in the thrashing rain and wind, I usually felt a little better. The fresh air and exercise weren't silver bullets for my problems, but the new addition to my daily routine soon became a lifeline, something that anchored me to a sense of normality. So every Saturday and Sunday I walked and walked, and walked, dreaming of a life where I could yomp through the countryside forever. Nature calmed my mind. The roaring sea gave me a place to dream. And every step made me feel briefly lighter, until around *Antiques Roadshow* o'clock, when Monday's heavy presence loomed large and the darkness hit again.

At first, I walked from my front door to Boscombe or Sandbanks. Later, once I'd become more committed, I took on much longer walks to Corfe Castle and Weymouth, eating nothing but a banana on a 10 to 12-hour walk because fasting was a great way to keep my head clear. Sometimes I'd get a train or a bus to wherever I was going and then walk all the way home. On other occasions, I'd do it in reverse. Whichever way I travelled, I made sure to move from coffee shop to coffee shop. I wasn't there for small talk or human connection; I was so low emotionally that I could barely look anyone in the eye, let alone strike up a meaningful conversation with a stranger. But the experience of buying a coffee kept me sane because it was some small sign that I was existing. On the really bad days, it was the only thing that got me out of bed in the morning. When I was wracked with depression, the thought of walking three, four or five kilometres to a coffee shop, even in the bollock-tightening cold, was often enough to get me outside. Those breaks became my safety net.

During his absent years, Dad had started another family, and while I wasn't exactly close with my stepbrothers, at some point the message must have got through to some of them that I was having a rough time. At the start of 2020, with the pandemic beginning its terrifying spread through Italy and talk of border closures dominating the media, one of them, Tom, came by for a chat. We took a drive to the cliffs and as we sat in the car, the rain drumming on the roof, he tried to dig into why I was feeling so miserable.

'I'm a failure, bro,' I said, the tears dribbling down my cheeks. 'Thailand was home. I don't want to be here. It sucks.'

'Why?' said Tom. 'What's so bad about it?'

I waved a hand at the deluge outside. 'I hate it. The weather. The people. *Everything.*'

But England wasn't the problem. I was. And my doomy mood had recently been heightened because I'd tracked down a few of the mates I'd left behind several years ago. According to social media, they were married, they ran businesses, and they had houses, kids, and pets. Why not me? I had nothing, or so I thought, and the depressing highlights reel of Other People's Successes had caused my FOMO to run rampant.

'Why am I such a fuck-up?' I moaned to Tom. 'Why can't I find my place here?'

'But you've done loads of cool things,' he said. 'The Marines. Afghanistan. *Shipwrecked.* Stuff I could never do. The only person stopping you is *you.* So, what do you want to do?'

I stared out of the car window, through the wet and the bleak. The sea was frothing and churning ahead.

'I want to walk and get paid for it.'

'Well, I don't think that's going to happen,' said Tom, matter of factly.

But he was wrong. I just didn't know it yet.

I'M GONNA BE

When I'd posted that video of me on the cliffs, living my best/ worst life, it had been a way of masking the painful truth. I wasn't celebrating the moment. I was on the verge of a breakdown and putting on a brave face. What I'd really needed was help, not likes or emojis, but without an idea of where to get it or how to ask for it, I was screwed until some lifeline arrived. Which it did, unexpectedly, a few minutes later when my phone buzzed with an alert from Instagram: *Rory has sent you a new message.* Trudging the path on my way to Corfe Castle, I didn't instantly register the note as being potentially life-changing because its sender was a person I hardly knew, like so many of my social media connections – a jumble of military colleagues, barely-there family members and total strangers. We'd been linked by the algorithm a few months earlier, and while there had been one or two likes and DMs (direct messages), Rory and I had never met in real life.

That made his message even more surprising.

@epic_origin_: I can see you walking around Great Britain. Then writing a book about it.

I later learned that Rory had been at home on his sofa watching a documentary about the world record-breaking swimmer Ross Edgley, the first person to swim around the British coastline, all 2,860 kilometres of it. When my video had appeared in his feed, he'd drawn a weird parallel that linked me and the man floating among the jellyfish on his TV.

The British seaside + a physical test = Paul.

Rory probably didn't believe that I'd take the suggestion seriously. But as I registered his message, my wheels began spinning. *Why couldn't I follow the same lines as Edgley? I thought.* A coastal walk around England, Wales and Scotland would be nowhere near as gruelling as a swim – or as dangerous, for that matter. Rory would later tell me that by the time Edgley's mission had been concluded, the arches in his feet were wrecked, part of his tongue had been disintegrated by salt water and his neck was so chafed by his wet suit that the skin became calloused.

I carried on walking, inspired by the idea. Then I remembered how Edgley's 'Great British Swim' had created a real sense of purpose – he'd wanted people to think of his efforts as evidence that anyone could do anything, especially if it was an act of mental and physical endurance. This was exactly the challenge I needed. Maybe I could be the *anyone* doing the *anything.* And then I felt the familiar tickle of butterflies in the pit of my stomach and realised I'd been dropped at an emotional crossroads, one we've all experienced: a moment when our gut tells us to go for a girl, a guy, a job or a weird adventure. At first, the stomach lurches with excitement as our brains urge us to make the leap, before the anxious energy turns to doubt, and we look to friends and family for reassurances. If my stepbrother was anything to go by, I wouldn't be getting much in the way of encouragement from that lot. But maybe I didn't need it?

The British coastline + a physical test = Me.

Everything was chiming.

I felt my strides quickening as my brain began to turn over. *So, what about the downsides?* Well, I'd have to quit my job and check out from The Real World for a year or so. *But who really gave a fuck about that?* I didn't have a lot of cash either, so I'd be surrendering myself to 'The Path' – a network of trails that framed the perimeter of the British Isles – probably by wild camping for a couple of years. From what I'd heard, homelessness wasn't much fun. It was also a long way to go, at least several thousand kilometres, taking into consideration the navigating of the wild Welsh coastline and the miles and miles of Scottish inlets. Then there was the British weather, which isn't known for its kindness in the summer, let alone winter. I consoled myself with the thought that if I went ahead with the idea, at least I wouldn't be developing rhino neck. Or losing half a tongue.

By the time I'd made it home to Bournemouth, I was halfway to the beginning of the making of a plan. Like Tom had suggested as we'd sat in his car on that miserable, rainy day, the only person who could potentially stop me from pressing ahead was me – not Dad, not my family and not my boss. To fire myself up even more, I recalled several bad life choices from my past and a long litany of regrets. There had been several occasions when I'd turned either left or right on a big decision, and in the messy aftermath, I'd wondered what might have happened had I gone the other way. Rory's challenge was such a moment and ignoring it would probably leave me in a bad place. I'd be haunted by doubts and regret for sure.

And yet my still mind flip-flopped. I thought about the roof over my head, the monthly wage and the three meals a day. The mental calculations were shaking me; I felt like a paperclip caught between two magnets, where one powerful force was a life of miserable certainty and the other a terrifying unknown.

Yes. *No.*

Course I am. *Course I'm not.*

I'm doing it. *This is so stupid.*

The turning point arrived shortly afterwards while visiting a mate, Emma. I was mid-wobble, snapped in two by yet another panic attack and barely clinging on. Having become concerned by my emotional state when we'd chatted on the phone, Emma had driven down to collect me so I could stay at her place in Basingstoke for a few restful days. The following morning, as she ran errands, I decided to go walking and I scrolled through Google Maps to find any points of interest. A pin marking a nearby Roman ruins appeared on the screen. The distance was a round trip of 25 kilometres, walkable, so I went for it, imagining myself stepping through a series of *Clash of the Titans*-style pillars, only to be met with several underwhelming mounds of dirt. But something about the place brought me back to Rory's message.

If I can find the energy of a warrior, then maybe I can do it, I thought, staring at the rocks and picturing the people who might have stuck them there in the first place.

I reached for my phone and called Emma. 'I'm fucking going for it,' I said. 'I'm going to be a warrior walker.'

Really, the decision to walk The Path wasn't mine to make. I like to think that it was a pre-destined and unavoidable call to action. I had to go, whether I liked it or not. And waiting for the perfect time was only going to prevent me from joining with my future self. Then I thought of the former Dorset resident Lawrence of Arabia. *This is the type of adventure he'd take.* If I didn't seize the moment, I'd spend the rest of my life an angry man, raging at the sea, having not grabbed my chance when there was absolutely nothing left to lose. That first rush of adrenaline at Rory's message had been my Lawrence of Arabia moment. A subconscious voice was telling me what to do. Or, to put it another way, it was the divining rod to a happier self. I only had to act on it to experience a better life, I was sure.

Within three weeks, I was packed and ready to go. I was joining The Path.

* * *

My first morning as the Warrior Walker was a vibes rollercoaster.

It was now the beginning of July 2020; the country had been in and out of lockdown for several months, but my plan was to complete the walk in around a year. Given all my military and contracting experience, when I'd spent several years walking for hours on end with a giant Bergen rucksack on my back, I reckoned I had it in me to yomp a marathon a day without too much bother. I'd also been trained to press ahead whatever the weather. The four tenets of the Royal Marine Code were courage, determination, unselfishness and cheerfulness in the face of adversity. Though given my emotional state, I wasn't entirely sure how the latter would stack up. Nor was Dad, who dropped a succession of hints about the impracticality of my decision as I packed and planned.

Fair point, I thought. I was going to be homeless for a year, maybe more. Respite from sleeping outdoors was going to be dependent on the love of a few old friends who lived close to the route. Some of them had said they were happy for me to crash on their sofas, when I told them of my expedition. Given all of that, I was prepared for every possible eventuality and packed enough clothes for four months of hot weather, four months of cold and four months of somewhere in-between. There was also a giant sleeping bag, some shower gel (two bottles) and plenty of toothpaste (two giant tubes). To weigh myself down even more, I even packed a book, *Can't Hurt Me: Master Your Mind and Defy the Odds*, by the former US Navy SEAL David Goggins. What I didn't have was a tent because I couldn't afford one, but I was confident of finding a dry spot to sleep in, no matter the weather. Other than that, there was no plan B, no fallback position and no reliable support to call upon. I wasn't a posh kid taking a risk, knowing I'd land softly in the event of a disaster. I was well and truly on my own, with only £300 in my pocket on which to survive.

Dad reminded me of that fact from the minute I quit my job. His prodding only intensified as my departure date approached.

'Is this supposed to be cool or something?' he said one morning, as I sat hunched over a map of Britain, trying to psychologically navigate all 1,014 kilometres of the South West Coast Path.

'No, it isn't,' I said. 'No one cares about walking . . . Why would they?'

'Well, what's the point then?' said Dad. I could tell he was frustrated.

'Because it's there. Because we're all going to die one day and if I don't do something like this, I'll be miserable about it for the rest of my life.'

'But that's the thing, isn't it? *This isn't life*. Life is going to work. It's about paying the bills. And maybe going on holiday once a year. That's it.'

I could feel my temper rising. 'No, it's not!' I snapped, folding away the map. 'You should wake up happy. You should wake up feeling passionate about something . . . Have a purpose. What you're talking about is *existing*. It's not *living*. And it's bloody miserable.'

Dad, to his credit, calmed down for a bit, but our truce was temporary. His final comment was saved for my last few minutes in the house as I struggled to the door, the overstuffed rucksack now slung around my shoulders.

'You don't have to do it, you know,' he said.

'*It?*'

'Yeah. *The walk*. You've made your point. No one will think anything less of you if you don't go ahead with this . . .'

I had no doubt that Dad was as likely relieved to see the back of me as I was of him, such was our troubled relationship.

But his negative presence also represented the last gatekeeper in a first-player video game. The big boss. The final villain. *Doubt*.

'Yeah, maybe they won't . . . But I will,' I said.

Despite our bickering, he kindly drove me down the road to Coast Café, a coffee shop in Poole, the starting point for my first day on The Path, where I'd arranged to meet a few mates. Among them was Tommy, a bloke I'd previously worked out with at a local gym, where we'd attempted to push, pull and sweat away our respective troubles. After each session, we'd spend a couple of hours slurping coffee and therapising ourselves. Alongside him at the table was my brother, Tom, and his wife.

Tommy was all smiles. A few weeks earlier, as we'd discussed my walks around the coast, he had made a suggestion: 'Mate, use your Instagram page as a journal. Just put stuff up every day. I reckon a few people are going to be interested in what you're doing.'

I shrugged. *Would they?* I doubted that, but not wanting to put a negative spin on what was a creative thought, I promised to commit to it, if only for him.

We drank coffee, laughed and ate cakes, until the moment to walk away became unavoidable. I felt my throat tightening. I couldn't delay the first steps any longer. The tears were coming. I grabbed my rucksack, its weight immediately biting into my back and shoulders.

Tommy hugged me tightly. 'You've got to go quick, mate,' he said. 'Otherwise, I'm going to cry.'

I felt instantly weakened by the love. *Maybe Dad is right? Maybe I don't have to leave?* Then someone waved to the girl behind the counter, who paused the music playing through the speakers. There was an awkward silence followed by a stampeding guitar riff that clattered around the room as a Scottish voice started singing about walking 500 miles. *Wait. I know this. The Proclaimers. That song.* It weirdly felt like a call to action, or some pivotal moment in a film. I stepped outside, into the hot sun, believing I was in the right place – taking my first steps on The Path to exactly where I needed to be. Probably for the first time ever.

CHAPTER FOUR

UNBURDENING

The first night was messy. The stag. That frantic jog to the church. My sleep punctuated by clanging bells. But as I laid on the stone paving and stared at the vast expanse of sky, the night became a hypnotic widescreen TV. Smudges of flickering pinpricks twinkled above me, thousands of glowing dots that faded in and out of view. Some of them seemed to pulse as tiny spectral heartbeats. Others played hide and seek with the cosmos, disappearing suddenly as if burned out before spluttering into life again. The size and scale of the universe made me feel minuscule, like I was a grain of sand on a beach, and I realised that in the grand scheme of things, my life and all the shit that came with it was a comma in a never-ending book of stories. But while my problems were insignificant compared to what was going on up there, they were still my problems and I had to tackle them, especially the physical ones, which were piling up at an alarming rate.

When morning came around, every part of me was in agony. My back ached. My calves burned. I felt the pull of muscle and ligament around my shoulders, ankles and knees. I hadn't managed more than 30 or 40 minutes' sleep in one go, and I was already exhausted.

Bloody hell, I thought. *I'm in bits and I've not been walking five minutes.*

The overwhelming sense that I might have bitten off more than I could chew was underlined when I grabbed my Bergen for the first full day of walking. It seemed so much heavier than before! I peered inside to make sure that Tommy hadn't added a few rocks for a laugh and saw the clump of winter clothes, shower gels and toothpastes. The burden was all mine. I readjusted the straps and sighed. Rather than sulking or stressing, I thought back to the parade square at Lympstone and my drill sergeant's suggestion that I should show cheerfulness in the face of adversity. *The fucker*. Smiling wasn't easy to do when groaning through a succession of push-ups but it had taught me that I could do hard things.

So I can handle this, I thought.

Striding back to the beach at Lulworth Cove, watching for more antlered monsters while wondering if their symbolic representation of strength, spiritualism and new journeys would come to anything, I stripped down to my underwear and took a dip in the sea. The icy cold slapped the air from my lungs and loosened my tense muscles.

I can figure this out.

Not ten minutes later, I was dressed and beginning the day's step count, where I briefly considered the solitary miles ahead.

The distance seemed daunting and I'd likely be walking with the demons of Thailand, Joy, and my shattered family life for company, all of them bouncing around in my head. That wouldn't make for a great headspace and the idea of experiencing another panic attack, alone and in the middle of nowhere, filled me with dread. Rather than wallowing in the anxiety of it all, I immediately challenged myself to greet every person I passed on the journey with a smile – no matter the weather or my mood. This was a big ask: any form of conversation on The Path would require me to step out of my comfort zone and into an awkward environment where I'd have to engage. *With strangers.* But it also seemed like robust defence mechanism and a small move towards being slightly less alone.

It'll keep you sane, I told myself.

And almost immediately, another walker appeared on the horizon.

At first, they were a small dot on a ghostly trail of flattened grass, sand and chalk that curved around a clifftop. The sea was whooshing and frothing to my left as a light mist burned away in the morning sun. The path ahead seemed to be shimmering and melting in the heat but as I walked, the small dot became two bigger dots, which then became a little old lady and her dog. As they got closer, I smiled nervously and waved, and was reminded of those defining opening moments in a job interview, where it was important to leave a good first impression. *Say something,* I told myself as she was almost passing by. *Get comfy with the weirdness.* Then I committed.

'Hey, how are you?' I said, almost apologetically, feeling my insides curdle.

The lady stopped. The dog sniffed around my pocket in a hunt for treats. 'Where are you going with that massive bag?' she said cheerily. She was wearing walking trousers, t-shirt and trainers. The wind buffeted her shoulder-length grey hair. I'd have put her at around 70 years old.

Here we go, I thought.

'OK . . . Well, long story short: I got a message from a friend to walk around Britain . . . So here I am.'

'Really?' she said. '*All of it?* That sounds a bit extreme.'

'Well, yeah. I guess it does.'

Deciding to take a breather, I loosened the Bergen, its unwieldy weight sliding to the floor. Then I delivered the highlights reel on my backstory in an emotional burp of crushing lows and mega-dramas: Mum, Dad, the Marines, Afghanistan, Thailand, Joy, the darkness. I don't think I stopped to ask the woman's name. I certainly don't recall it now. But as I spoke, she nodded sympathetically. I sensed she wasn't going to criticise me. Even if she did, I wasn't likely to see her again, so it didn't really matter. Moments later, we were perched on a nearby bench and I was sobbing into her shoulder. The tears came in floods, I couldn't stop, and I realised it was the first time I'd ever fully unloaded my unhappiness onto another person. It had only ever been done in fits and starts before because I'd been so scared of judgement – from my peers, my brothers, even Dad.

'For my whole life, I haven't felt good enough,' I said.

I'd never been one for therapy. Even telling Tommy about the dark enormity of my problems, in full, had been impossible because I'd previously worked in a highly masculine environment where any issues were either laughed away or buried.

I was learning that the problem with bottling things up was that it added pressure to the pain, especially when there was no lid to twist, or pop off. The emotional upset had to escape somehow and when it did, there was usually an eruption. In some people, it manifested itself in violence or an outbreak of destructive behaviour. In others, the result was a panic attack or a flood of tears on a coastal path with a total stranger and her dog.

The waterworks, and the release that came with them, felt weirdly uplifting. As I cried, I realised the lady had carried no preconceptions about me – and she would have been forgiven for experiencing a few. After all, I was a burly, ex-Marine, trudging along on an isolated stretch of the trail, and she was a pensioner. From a distance, I must have cut an intimidating figure. But instead of avoiding me or making a series of assumptions about who I was, or what I was doing, she had stopped to talk. This realisation pushed all my reticence aside and I started blurting out my fears, one by one: that I was worried I'd never find the happiness I'd experienced in Thailand; that my chances of a fulfilling family life had gone for ever; that I'd never meet another person like Joy.

And then there was the elephant in the room.

'I'm walking because I've got no choice,' I snotted loudly.

'What makes you say that?' she said. 'There's always a choice.'

Unable to hold back, I whispered the scariest truth of all: 'Yeah. Maybe. But sometimes I don't want to be here anymore. And this might be the only way to save myself from a horrible ending.'

Just saying those words aloud felt awkward and humbling

and unnatural. But I was being honest – to a total stranger, who became the very first person to see the real me.

'Oh, Paul. You poor thing . . .' she said.

The woman listened to the final instalment of my story – the walk, my first night on The Path with the stag and the church yard. Then she squeezed me tightly. 'You're doing something truly wonderful.'

'I feel so embarrassed, crying like this,' I said, wiping away the wet and gloop from my cheeks and nose.

'Don't. *Please*. You should feel good about it. *About you*.' The lady gestured to the hilly route winding around the coast. It looked like an impenetrable mountain range. 'It's very brave. Not many people would even try it.'

Then she rummaged around in her pocket and grabbed my hand. I felt a crumpled note being pressed into my palm.

'Here's a tenner.'

'*What?* No! You don't have to do—'

'Yes, I do. The next place you stop, get a coffee and a cake on me. I'm very proud of you . . .'

Then I cried again. She reminded me of Nan.

* * *

After walking for a couple of days, I'd made the smallest of dents in the South West Coast Path, the 1,014-kilometre stretch of undulating tracks that edges the shores of Somerset, Devon, Cornwall and Dorset. My home in Bournemouth was somewhere near to the famous route's start line – or the finish, depending on where you began the journey. But whichever way you cut it, the effort to get round was known to be daunting.

A lot of people tackle the South West Coast Path every year and wild campers are a familiar sight on the trail, especially in the summer. So I wasn't exactly an outlier on The Path – even during the middle of a pandemic – and it wasn't uncommon to see a tent pitched on the headlands or clifftops. As I passed people, they made cheery comments about me tackling one of the UK's most famous walks. When I then explained that the South West Coast Path was a small fraction of my overall target, they looked at me like I was mad.

This reaction was amplified by what was going on at the time. Despite the beautiful July weather, Covid was still running rampant through the country. There was an air of paranoia to every encounter. People freaked out over hand sanitiser. A lot of conversations took place at a distance. And in every coffee shop or newsagent, customers were divided by plastic screens, barriers and signs that warned of the dangers of close contact. While outdoor exercise was now being permitted, the mood around the country was divided on who should be doing what and when, and there was a good chance I might incur the wrath of some busybody. But seeing as there were far more important things for everybody to be worrying about, I pressed ahead. My guess was that on most days I'd encounter more seagulls than humans.

While I walked, I posted pictures, videos and the odd update on social media – not for clicks, but because it would make for a diary of sorts. After the confusing, often unwelcome recognition that followed *Shipwrecked*, the idea of being a big-time influencer didn't feel too appealing. The most important thing was that I was talking. I hashtagged every message and picture like a low-key version of Ross Edgley in the hope that someone in a similar emotional hole to me might feel inspired, as I had been by him. Every new follower gave me a glimmer of hope but, at the same time, the attention also freaked me out. *How are a few hundred people interested in me?* I thought one morning, staring at my phone. It all seemed so weird. An old mate from school said hello. One or two colleagues from the military checked in. I got into a routine whereby every morning, I updated my page by detailing where I was, where I'd slept and how I felt. (Achy, tired, confused, mainly.) The positive feedback, when it came, was nice.

Then life became surreal.

I was stepping past Weymouth when a DM appeared. It was a stranger with a weird question:

Hey, Warrior Walker!

Is getting you a room a thing? Because I would love to treat you to a hotel one night. My friend Ross has a favourite hotel near to where you are. It's called The Bull in Bridport.

Sarah

I felt instantly confused. Red flags flapped; alarm bells clanged; all the Spidey senses tingled. *Who offers a 'thing' like a free hotel room to a random walker on the internet?* More importantly, while the gesture was incredibly kind, I had no idea who she was. My mind went to the dark places. Everybody knew that backpackers made for easy prey in horror movies. Hitchhikers and hillwalkers too. Meanwhile, the South West Coast Path was just about the perfect place to hide a corpse. *So, was this a trap?*

I scrolled through Sarah's socials and checked her admittedly friendly-looking photos for any signs of malevolent intent. Having decided that she was the kind-hearted type and realising I was in desperate need of a good night's rest, I messaged back – but cautiously. *I can always block her if she sounds like the next Rose West or Josef Fritzl,* I thought.

'Hey. I'm not sure what you mean?'

Moments later, Sarah was explaining how she'd stumbled across my Instagram account. After following my posts for a few days and having left several encouraging posts, plus one or two thumbs-up emojis, she'd decided I needed a helping hand.

Still feeling unsure, I took some time to mull the offer over. So far, the British summer had been amazing. But while I was roasting during the day, the nights were becoming increasingly cold and damp, and it was only a matter of time before an unexpected storm or temperature drop wiped me out for a few days, especially as I was still camping without a tent. Eventually, I looked at the map. Bridport wasn't that far away and at my speed, I'd likely be tucked up in a cosy bed by nighttime. Realising that the pros of taking up Sarah's offer were heavily outweighing the cons, I decided to go for it.

Why not? 'Yeah! That's an amazing gesture,' I typed. 'If that's OK?'

Once the details had been confirmed, I walked past Abbotsbury and its famous swan sanctuary, scrabbling for hours across a pebble beach that sucked me to the floor like quicksand. I felt a little guilty for not sleeping on The Path, but just imagining the stack of fluffed pillows, a warm shower and a full English breakfast at The Bull kept me going until I'd neared Bridport. Then my heart sank. To reach my destination, I'd have to climb to the top of a steep road and it looked a million miles away. Feeling defeated, I briefly fantasised about booking a train to Bournemouth for the following morning. After all, I'd already done enough to earn the respect of Tommy and one or two others. (Though probably not Dad.) So why not go home?

I was fading. A weird sense of imposter syndrome crept up on me, almost from out of nowhere and I thought of other lads I knew, peers from the military, that had followed their service with acts of epic bravery. They'd climbed Death Zone mountains. They'd trekked across deserts. And they'd rowed vast expanses of ocean, sometimes unsupported. My walk suddenly felt small-time in comparison.

Sighing, I recognised these emotions for what they really were. My frazzled brain was trying to give my body a break. Meanwhile, the looming sense of imposter syndrome represented an understandable moment of self-doubt. Reaching for clarity, I told myself that everything was relative and given my fragile emotional state, The Path represented a psychological battle as big as any ocean row or desert trek – my emotional Himalayas and Karakoram rolled into one. The covered distances, altitude, and gradient didn't matter. My push to The Bull Hotel was the first big emotional test in a very long journey, and I had no choice but to face up to it. By giving up now, I'd be tumbling back to square one and my old life, where I'd likely end up in a very bad place.

Then I remembered back to my Royal Marines training days, when an exercise or drill was unexpectedly extended by several hours. Back then, the instructors had wanted to instil another layer of resilience into us, while delivering a lesson on the horrific realities of warfare. The message: *There was always one more hill, Marine.*

So, gritting my teeth, I trudged upwards.

Oh no, I thought, staring at what felt like a sheer incline. *Here we go.*

When I eventually arrived at the check-in desk, a 20-something-year-old woman looked at me and squealed. I'd never known anyone so excited to see me.

'Oh my god, you're the Warrior Walker!' she said, introducing herself as the hotel manager. 'Ross told us about you. I checked your page. I love what you're doing!'

She then explained that the room was indeed paid for, as was my breakfast. Even better, the hotel staff had decided to shout my dinner.

'There's a pizza oven in the connecting restaurant,' said the hotel manager. 'Order whatever you want and make sure to take a second one.'

I wanted to check for hidden cameras. *Is this a wind up?* I thought. I felt like a competition winner and became immediately suspicious.

'A second one,' I said. '*Why?*'

'Well, for later,' said the hotel manager, like it was the most obvious thing in the world. Then she pulled down a door key and showed me to my room.

I couldn't get my head around it. More unexpected acts of generosity from strangers had come my way in the past few days than in an entire lifetime. An old lady had shoved a tenner into my hand. Now this: a hotel room paid for by somebody I'd never met and with the promise of free pizzas from the staff.

None of these people had been expected to help but they'd done so anyway, because they wanted to. Just for the sake of it. When I saw my room, a four-poster bed at one end, a standing bath and coffee machine at the other, I fell onto the mattress and sobbed into the luxurious display pillow, convinced I was seeing the best of humanity, wondering what the hell I'd done to deserve it.

'Thank you, strangers on the internet,' I mumbled, trying not to leave a damp blob on the fabric. 'Thank you. Thank you. *Thank you.*'

CHAPTER FIVE

BLOOD OF THE STONE

I walked the next day, a cold, leftover pizza in my bag, and imagined a weird union being formed: me and The Path. Because it was starting to feel like a constant companion, one that didn't care whether I was happy or sad and didn't judge. No matter the weather, it arced around the coastline and I only had to put one foot in front of the other to make progress. Whenever I felt alone, I stared at the sea on my left for company. *Always on my left*. On sunny days, it seemed to twinkle all around me. Wherever I looked at the track ahead it reminded me of the enormity of my journey and my place in the world. When the waves smashed into the cliffs with an explosion of battleship grey and white foam, I accepted my powerless position, knowing that I'd become part of something much bigger than myself. And that was everything. At my unhappiest, I'd been a slave to technology, stuck indoors and chained to my phone, pretending that the relationships contained inside it were genuine. Yeah, my job gave me a monthly wage; there had been some benefits and a little security. But I'd been bloody miserable. By walking around Great Britain with a rucksack on my back, the sea at my side and a friendly face or two along the trail, I was connecting.

So far, the South West Coast Path had been a daunting test. Not only was it over 1,014 kilometres long – and I was only around 20 per cent of the way around – but it was also an undulating monster that snaked down to sandy beaches and climbed to the top of tall cliffs. At times, the route ahead of me looked like a Blackpool rollercoaster.[1]

Every hill was a battle, particularly when the sun was at its highest and I was out of water, with no beach café or coffee shop in sight. On those occasions, I did my best to stay positive. Having crested a hill, I rewarded myself with some congratulatory words. Then I reset and went again, savouring the downhill slopes and preserving my energy for the next ascent.

Whenever a climb felt too daunting, or the steps ahead seemed too painful, I minimised the task into bitesize chunks. The next footfall. The next breath. The next beach. *One more hill*, I told myself at the foot of every vertiginous climb. I remained present by remembering I only had one set of ankles, one set of knees and one set of feet, so I had to watch where I was walking. Focusing on the movements in my limbs and the crunch of sand, grass and gravel beneath my trail shoes helped to silence the doubts whenever they called from the darkness.

---

1   A fellow walker would later tell me over coffee that the gradients of the South West Coast Path, when tallied up, were three times greater than those of Mount Everest. I have no idea how accurate the statistic is, but it was hard to put up a decent counterargument, given the pain in my body.

There were downers, of course. Sometimes, during a long period of solitude, when I didn't pass another person for hours, my emotional baggage felt heavier than the Bergen. I wondered what the hell I was doing with my life and whether anyone cared. In the middle of nowhere, unseen by anyone, I could have disappeared off the nearest cliff without another soul knowing. In such an emotional hole, moving forward was the biggest obstacle of all.

So how much do I want it?

Quite a lot, as it turned out.

Whenever I walked near to a Roman or Viking historical site, of which there were a few along The Path, I was reminded of my inspirational journey to Basingstoke (of all places) and my sense of union with a long-buried lineage of travellers and pioneers. Whether it was a protected mound of earth on the landscape, the sign of some ancient burial ground, or the crumbling skeleton of an ancient villa or monument, the energy reminded me of my purpose: to keep exploring, because that's what the old warriors had done, not knowing what was over the horizon. Meanwhile, I had a portable wardrobe on my back, a satellite assisted mapping system in my pocket (plus an old school paper version, just in case), and a direct link to the nearest doctor, should I break an ankle or go down with a burst appendix. At times it felt like cheating.

Since leaving Bournemouth, I'd walked between 25 kilometres and a marathon a day, depending on my mood. The long summer sunsets meant I could yomp at night, a headtorch illuminating the route ahead when the moon wasn't bright enough. While walking, I liked to chat with the universe, taking rough guesses as to the time and date by looking at the stars or checking whether the moon was waxing or waning, and my estimates were becoming increasingly accurate. Like a maritime sailor, albeit a couple hundred years out of time, I was dialling into Mother Nature and all her clues, planning my movements through the orbiting planets and churning tides. It made me feel more human than ever.

I was beginning to spot the warning signs that sometimes predicted what was happening beyond the immediate horizon, or around the next cove or bay. When my first summer storm whipped in, I sensed its presence well ahead of time, my skin goose-bumping at an almost imperceptible drop in temperature, as my nostrils caught the first whiff of petrichor, or 'the blood of the stone'. This aroma of soil bacteria and plant oils mixed with the sharp, metallic charge of lightning and ozone hinted at an impending downpour. It's claimed that humans can detect petrichor like sharks can sniff blood in the water – we were once finely attuned to it – which was a very useful resource when walking the British coast.

At the first sign, I tightened my coat and waited for the skies around me to bruise. Then I walked into the blast and imagined that the water soaking my cheeks was an emotional carwash. *It's there to sloosh away the pain*, I told myself, the rain dripping from my nose. In the Marines, I'd learned to survive in the cold and the wet. On The Path, I was learning to thrive in it, and I soon came to trust my instincts more and more. Forget looking at a weather app. From then on, I checked the skies around me, sniffed the air for petrichor and left the rest to fate. The philosopher Jon Kabat-Zinn once said that while it isn't possible to control the waves, it is possible to surf. The South West Coast Path seemed about the best place to put that theory into practice, and a summer shower soon came to feel like joy because I was moving with it, accepting the cold and wet, rather than fighting to defeat an invincible enemy.

The sun seemed just as connecting. In the early morning, the coast was often shrouded in a heavy, swirling fog. It hung above the water and clung to the clifftops. When the day moved on and the sun climbed higher, that gloom faded away into a silvery mist. By midday, with the heat radiating on my back and face, everything became easier. My strides seemed lighter; I felt hopeful about my progress; gratitude washed over me like waves. For The Path. For the kestrels spiralling above. Even for the scalding winds that whiplashed off the water. In a few months, once autumn had frozen into early winter, the cold and wet would become a ferocious force. I knew that, with hindsight, my first few weeks of walking would seem like a picnic. I made sure to savour the moment.

When it's pissing down, you'll kill for days like this . . . I told myself, imagining the future storms with a shiver. Then I signed into the hotspots around me – the tide shattering on the coastline, the sea breeze gossiping through the long grass, the seagulls pecking at a bag of abandoned chips on a promenade. This was living.

* * *

Something weird was happening too. Sarah's message, Ross's favourite hotel, the old lady and her dog: these weren't glitches or bugs in The Path's programming. They were features, and more people wanted to connect with me online and in real life.

An elderly walker sat patiently on a bench. As I hustled into view, a bundle of fast-moving limbs, facial hair and sweat, he waved out.

'Are you the Warrior Walker?' he said, inviting me to sit by him for a chat. 'I've heard about you on my phone.'

On other sections of the coastal trail, total strangers arrived with coffee and homemade sarnies. Some of them even offered to join me as a temporary walking companion. My Instagram reach was expanding and everyone I spoke to wanted to help in some way, which was a completely different vibe to the world I was seeing through the news headlines, where, according to 'experts on the internet', the country was being divided along several distinct and violent battlelines. The Brexit vote, Covid, the toxic influence of Donald Trump and a looming cost-of-living crisis, not to mention several culture wars over gender, sexuality, race and religion. Every time I caught a snippet of the news or a glimpse of morning telly in a coffee shop, Great Britain seemed to be at war with itself.

My lived reality was telling a very different story, though. On The Path, people were good. People were kind. People didn't care who I voted for or whether I believed the coronavirus had started naturally or was part of the Great Reset – whatever that was. I was bulletproof to all the nonsense because I didn't have a job, I didn't have a house and I didn't have any security, which made me less susceptible to the type of fearmongering and pressures peddled by the everyday news. Instead, my circumstances had placed me in direct contact with human nature – face to face, rather than in a Twitter rant – where every story and perspective seemed authentic. Chatting to strangers brought a boost of positive affirmation and I felt heard. I was also able to hear others. My phone chimed with messages from old mates and the announcement of another new follower on Instagram. There were lots of supportive messages from strangers. But nothing from Dad.

There's a saying that suggests we are the five people we spend the most time with. So, if a person spends their life with five negative souls, well, guess what? They'll become the sixth. Walking The Path through early July showed me that there were only two types of people, the drains and the radiators, and I had to be careful which ones I connected with. The drains were energy vampires: the online cynics, trolls and pessimists. (Though you could find them IRL too, if you looked hard enough.) They had the potential to suck the life out of a moment or conversation. The radiators, on the other hand, were people with the power to transmit love, generosity and kindness. I very much saw myself as the latter and did my best to express humanity to every walker I met. As a result, empathy and altruism beamed back at me a hundredfold, and with every *hello* and hug, I experienced a huge rush of endorphins. It numbed the aching in my back, feet and calves, and silenced the negative self-talk. I walked a little bit taller too.

Maybe Dad not calling is for the best, I thought, a little sadly. (But not too sadly.)

Then, one morning, I looked at the map and realised I was yomping towards Lympstone, the location of my 32 weeks of basic training and emotional hell with the Royal Marines.

One of my good friends from 40 Commando, a bootneck called Simon Stroud – or Stroudy as he was known – had already checked in with an invitation. He was 20 years into a regimental career and knew about my situation through someone on social media. He wanted to know if I was coming onto the base. Even though I knew I'd be passing by, the thought of going back hadn't crossed my mind. *Would I even be allowed?* Surely, I needed an ID card of some kind to be granted access.

'I don't know . . .' I typed.

Stroudy sounded surprised, '*You don't know?* How could you not?'

'I left years ago. Can I even get in?'

'Come on Royal,' he said. 'You're with me.'

When I eventually arrived and walked past the training centre's famous assault course, I saw several grim-faced recruits. Then I stepped into the drill sergeant's office where Stroudy now conducted his business and everything flashed back at me all at once. As he stepped around his desk to shake my hand, I saw the starchy fabric of his uniform, smelt the mustiness of military housekeeping and noticed that very little had changed in my 20-year absence. I was instantly jolted back to my 18-year-old self, with all those insecurities, fears and vulnerabilities.

I'd been a nightmare recruit back then and spent the first few weeks crying myself to sleep because I was unable to press my kit and sheets to the required standard. The anxiety of being beasted by a drill sergeant was so overwhelming, I sometimes slept on the floor to prevent my bedding from becoming overly crumpled. But with time, the hurricane in my mind settled to a mild storm. My confidence grew with every training drill.

When I visited home during Christmas leave, a lot of the girls in town noticed me, probably for the very first time, because I was a Marine and leaner and fitter and bloody hench. I even thought about jacking in the military because I was having so much fun on civvy street. Booze. Parties. And a whole lot more.

Having made up my mind to quit, a commanding officer listened to what was a half-arsed resignation speech. Then he sighed. He'd heard it all before. 'I'm not going to accept your decision today, Recruit Harris,' he said. 'I will tomorrow. But there's one condition.'

'Yes, sir?'

'Call someone you love and tell them what you're thinking. If you still want to leave after that, you can.'

Feeling confused, I rang my grandad and told him of my plans to come home.

'If that's what's going to make you happy, then fine,' he said. 'But do you want to be known as Paul Harris or Marine Harris?' he said.

My mind did a handbrake turn. Back then, Paul Harris was a nobody but Marine Harris had prospects, a future and potential hero status. I withdrew my resignation and cracked on with the training, passing out into the Royal Marines in March 2003 before serving in places I couldn't have imagined visiting as a scared, shy little kid. Like Iraq, Northern Ireland, Dubai, Sardinia and Columbia, where I very nearly died at a checkpoint while off duty. The story was all chaos: one night I'd stepped off the beaten track with friends to look for a casino, but we were clocked by four cartel-connected coppers, hauled from our car and shoved against the bonnet. I felt the cold metallic snub of a 9mm pistol being pressed into the back of my skull. At the time, my detail was to protect Merchant Navy ships from marauding pirates and murderous drug gangs, and it was a risky business. Getting shot on a jolly felt like a weird way to go.

Suddenly, a van pulled up alongside us. The driver was a local cleaner from our ship and he must have seen the kerfuffle unfolding on the roadside.

'You can't kill them,' he yelled out in Spanish. 'They're Royal Marines. It will make a big problem for you.'

Reluctantly, the dodgy cops released us unscathed. But not before taking all our cash. It was a sign I had to get out and it wasn't long before I was making my excuses and leaving the Armed Forces behind me.

That was two decades ago and I was a very different person, but Stroudy hadn't changed one bit. He was eyeing my Bergen suspiciously.

'What have you got in there? You climbing Everest . . . *twice?*'

I shuffled my feet nervously. 'I know,' I sighed, feeling embarrassed about the two tubes of toothpaste, two bottles of shower gel and a barely touched copy of David Goggins' *Can't Hurt Me.* 'You couldn't do a kit muster for me, could you? I don't know what to lose and what to keep.'

A kit muster is a military inspection in which the contents of a Marine's Bergen is assessed for the mission ahead. Unsure of what to expect on The Path, I'd stuffed my life's contents inside the bag, not knowing if I had over- or under-packed. I felt like a teenager going to his first ever Glastonbury, minus the Rizlas and magic mushrooms.

Stroudy laughed. 'I certainly can, Marine Harris. But you'll have to give me 30 push-ups in return.'

The look on his face told me he wasn't kidding. As I worked through a short set, my kit was pulled apart, Stroudy frowning at the scattered innards. He then dangled a pair of winter trousers in front of my face as I recovered.

'Why have you got these? It's bloody *summer*.'

By the end of his assessment, my bag had been stripped of weight. In the discard pile were those two bottles of shower gel, one large tube of toothpaste, several heavy jumpers and a woolly hat. The considerably lighter bag was shoved back at me. Stroudy smiled. It was a sunny August day. The recruits outside were smashing through drills in the heat. Twenty years previously, I'd been at my physical peak and performing feats of strength that now felt like a distant memory. Me racing over the assault course. Me standing proudly on parade. Me completing a 30-mile yomp while carrying full battle order. The energy of my past life unexpectedly filled me with excitement. As we walked to the mess hall, Stroudy introduced me as a Royal Marine to every person we met. Then he explained what I was doing. He sounded proud.

'You're going to smash this,' he said eventually. 'I know you are.'

The emotion swirled in my chest. I looked at him in his uniform and shiny boots and realised that the only memento from my time with the Royals Marines was a green beret, but I'd lost it.

'I miss that thing, man,' I said, pointing to the one on his desk as I later gathered up my stuff to leave.

'What do you mean? Where's yours?'

I nodded. 'Gone. In the madness of life, moving all over the place . . . I don't know where it is.'

Stroudy gave me a friendly shove. 'Well, once you've walked Britain, you can come back here for a replacement.'

'Yeah?'

He laughed. 'Yeah. Because you'll have bloody earned it, Marine Harris.'

THE ALMOST UNBEARABLE KINDNESS OF STRANGERS

After just over a week, I was some way along the East Devon coast. The route had taken me past Budleigh Salterton to the mouth of the River Exe, where I left the coastal path and followed the estuary inland towards Exeter. The route had taken me past Budleigh, before turning inland along the River Exe's estuary mouth, where I was pointed towards Exeter. Despite my brief hotel stay in Bridport, just over a week in, I needed another rest. Emotionally I was frazzled; I was so separated from domesticity that the sensation of warm running water or the soft luxury of proper toilet paper felt like a distant memory. My early-morning sea dips, while an invigorating kickstart to the day, weren't exactly relaxing. I was constantly on the lookout for walkers as I stripped out of my clothes. Then, having submerged to my shoulders, I'd watch anxiously for any potential bag thieves coming down the beach. Vigilance became my default setting during these moments when I was exposed and vulnerable, and I felt increasingly appreciative for the securities I'd once enjoyed at home.

When I moved, my darker thoughts were always close by, especially self-doubt, which re-emerged as I approached Exeter. On the trail, a sinister voice seemed to whisper to me from the shadows. It wanted me to quit. *There's a station nearby. You're only two hours from home on a train . . .*

Dad's voice rebounded back at me from a few weeks earlier: *You don't have to do it, you know.*

And then, finally: *This isn't real life.*

With each flicker of insecurity, I reminded myself that every step forward was an achievement. And that I had a real sense of purpose for the first time in forever.

There was also something to look forward to in Exeter. Mark called, a friend I'd worked with in Kabul, and told me he'd paid for a room in a fancy city centre hotel – the type of place visited by business types and American tourists. I couldn't believe my luck. Kipping rough was becoming increasingly painful and I craved the comforts of a warm bed. Mark's gesture arrived at just the right time. But when I entered the hotel's fancy foyer with its lush potted plants, shimmering floor tiles and a soundtrack of jazzy muzak, the woman at the counter looked at me in shock. Wild campers weren't the typical clientele, obviously, and I was covered in sand and grime. I probably smelled awful. She pointed to my heavy bag as it fell to the floor with a loud thud.

'What . . . what have you been *doing*?' she said.

I delivered an edited version, minus the tears. The receptionist looked flummoxed.

'Oh my god,' she said, waving to a nearby cart stacked with room service items. 'Take whatever you want from that. It sounds like you might need it.'

I gawped at the shelves of crisps, chocolate bars and bottled water and salivated. I was starved. 'Thanks,' I said, praying Mark's booking had gone through as promised. 'A mate of mine has paid for the room. It's for one night?'

The receptionist scanned her computer screen and nodded. Then she began typing frantically.

'It's all here, Mr Harris . . . And I seem to have upgraded you to a king-size room. Oops!'

Oops? I couldn't believe the generosity. *How come?*

'It's the pandemic,' she said, shrugging and handing me a room card. 'We're quiet. Nobody's going to notice because there's nobody here.'

I was stunned. Fearing a sudden change of heart, I quickly grabbed some supplies and stumbled towards my room, eating as I walked. The shower was incredible. I felt swaddled in the bed's duvet and pillows. My body, overcooked from the sweltering sun, began to cool. But the comforts of a city centre hotel soon lulled me into a false sense of security and when I woke the next day, my aches and pains felt a hundred times worse. I could barely move. Rather than soothing away the hurt, Mark's gift had reminded me of what I was missing out on, and when I stood up, every muscle groaned. But my mind was melting down too.

I felt another sharp pang of guilt for sleeping in a hotel room. *Is this cheating?*

FOMO kicked in soon after. *You've got to walk, bro*, said the voice. *You've got to keep going.*

I showered again and got dressed, not knowing that the universe had rearranged my schedule once more. When I limped through the foyer for breakfast, the same receptionist waved me over.

'Mr Harris, you've had your stay extended,' she said. 'So don't stress about checking out today if you don't want to.'

I still have no idea whether it was an act of generosity on her part or if Mark had come through for me yet again. But it couldn't have happened at a better time. I was close to broken.

Exeter is a beautiful city, encircled by remnants of Roman walls and defined by its Gothic architecture. Even in its guise as an abandoned, dystopian ghost town in the middle of a pandemic, it still carried a quiet grandeur. From my window, I could see the spindly turrets and ancient stonework of the city's famous cathedral. The streets were eerily empty – other than one or two dogwalkers – and I realised that I had the freedom of the place. Everyone else was working from home, which made it just about the best time imaginable to go sightseeing. Still feeling guilty about being briefly separated from The Path, I decided to make something of the day and strolled towards the cathedral's grand entrance. When I stepped inside, everything became still. Even the voices.

The building was a masterpiece. Its ceiling, woven together by a series of interlocking arches – skeletal fingers that steepled upwards – glowed brightly from several beams of multicoloured light. The illuminations bled from a line of stained-glass windows set into every wall. Dust motifs smoked through the air, creating a spectral vibe, and I was weirdly reminded of the light shows from some of the raves I'd gone to in the 1990s, where the dancefloor had pulsed under a blitz of lasers and dry ice. The silence felt off balance too. I was so used to the smash of the sea and the wash of the wind that whenever I stepped into somewhere more human, like a coffee shop, with its frothing machines and grinding beans, I was jolted towards real life – sometimes aggressively. But in the cathedral, there was nothing but serenity and I was instantly cocooned. My blood pressure dropped. I felt my lungs fill with air. One or two people walked by in masks and waved. Despite the brutal heatwave outside, a cool breeze drifted through the building, and the flagstone floor and stone pillars were cold to the touch. I was soothed. *Safe.*

Traditional religion wasn't really my thing, though I certainly believed in the idea of a higher power – whether that was nature, the universe or some mystical god, I wasn't sure. I was also fascinated by the eternal question of meaning and who we were. (And like everyone: *what was the bloody point of it all?*) If faith presented someone with a positive sense of purpose, or if it encouraged them to be kind and caring, then I was OK with it. But when the beliefs of an individual, or a collective, led them to violence, I struggled to understand the point. I also knew that when my time came, I'd probably end up praying. *Because we all do.* Aeroplane turbulence had shown me that. The idea of believing in something bigger than ourselves comes to us all at one point or another.

Something about religious buildings intrigued me too. Whenever I passed a temple in Thailand and noticed the Buddhist monks meditating, I stepped inside to soak up the silence. Every time I saw a church or cathedral on holiday, I looked around. Sometimes the art inside was like a collection from a famous gallery; the architecture was jaw-dropping; the experience brought me a weird sense of inner peace. Exeter Cathedral was no different.

After a few minutes of taking in the shimmering, summery light cascading through the rafters, I spotted a small room at the back of the main hall. Inside, a few people were sitting on pews as a priest led them in prayers. Carefully, I took a seat at the back and closed my eyes. I heard soothing murmurings and mumbled 'amens'.

I'm unsure of how long I sat there for. It might have ten minutes; it might only have been 60 seconds. But eventually, a whispered voice nearby announced that the cathedral was closing. Rising from my seat, I nearly fell backwards into someone standing behind me. When I turned, a kind-faced man in his sixties was looking at me. He was short, slight and balding. A pair of thin-rimmed glasses wobbled on his nose. Then I noticed the black and white flash of his priest's collar underneath a dark pullover.

'Did you enjoy prayers?' he said, smiling.

I was a little taken aback. 'Yeah, I did,' I said, feeling instantly self-conscious, as if I'd been caught with my hand in a biscuit tin. Having come face to face with another church-going person, a priest of all people, I felt exposed. My guard came up. The old Paul rushed back: a ten-year-old boy, quiet and withdrawn, with nothing to say and a whole load of regrets and anxieties weighing him down. I was out of place and wobbly. Sensing my unease, the priest seemed to adjust his whole aura.

'So, what brought you in here today?' he said, his voice dropping to an almost-whisper. 'Sightseeing? Or something else?'

I sighed. *Definitely something else.* I told him my name, my story and my plan to walk around the British coast in under a year. I then explained how I'd already walked around the edges of south Dorset and some of Devon since I'd started and was planning to complete Cornwall, North Devon and Somerset at a similar speed. The priest nodded, listening intently.

'So, you're on a pilgrimage then?'

I shook my head. 'No,' I said. 'Well . . . *maybe*? Depends on what that means.'

The priest ushered me out of the prayer room and into the main hall. The building was empty now. The last of the visitors had gone and the cathedral was even calmer and cooler than before. Pointing to a series of engraved plaques on a nearby stone wall, the priest indicated an inscription. When I looked, I noticed it was in Latin: *Memento mori.*

'Do you know what that represents?' he said.

I nodded. Sort of.

'It means, "Remember you must die." You're on a journey, whether you know it or not. In life. In faith. Your walk . . .'

He then told me about the Franciscan Way – the spiritual path inspired by St Francis of Assisi, the thirteenth-century Catholic friar who lived simply and devoted himself to peace, humility, poverty and a love of nature. These were values

I could connect with. I felt myself steadying. The emotional wall was lowering.

'I like that. But . . .'

The priest smiled. 'But?'

'But . . . religion. I almost fight it, especially if it's being forced on me. I'm not saying that it is now, it's just how I've felt in the past. I think I've given up on it.'

'Why?'

'I've seen so much. War. Mates killed in the Marines. A bloke murdered by the Taliban in Afghanistan. And now Covid. If religion's real, that wouldn't be happening, would it?' I checked myself finally. 'Sorry, I don't want to cause offence or anything.'

'None taken,' said the priest. 'But it seems as if you have a whole path to explore. Maybe you can find the answers you're looking for there.'

Then he shook my hand. 'You're going to be all right, Paul,' he said finally. 'Go well. And seize the day.'

When I stepped outside, into the bright light, the calm of the cathedral seemed to fade away. I felt my purpose moving into view.

CHAPTER SEVEN

A POSTCARD FOR THE UNIVERSE

I hadn't needed an old lady to shove a tenner into my hand; I hadn't needed a receptionist to give me free snacks in an Exeter hotel and I hadn't needed a priest to validate my actions. But, bloody hell, it had felt good to receive the supportive gestures and I appreciated every single one of them. They also led me to an interesting thought: given that these events had all been happy accidents, and entirely unexpected, what would happen if I asked the universe for help directly? Might more fortuitous encounters come my way or would I jinx a lucky streak?

I first tested the idea as I continued to push around the pointy, calloused toes of England's south west, past Torquay, Salcombe and Mevagissey. The walk was brutal and as a succession of hills slowed my pace, a brutal wind whipped off the sea. Squalls of sand and dust scraped at my skin and eyes as I reached Carne Beach, and with nowhere to hide, I settled into a fox hole and waited for the worst to pass. It was late afternoon. I hadn't yet spotted a suitable sleeping place and my anxiety was peaking. Rolling over, I looked skyward.

'I need a room for the night!' I screamed.

If the cosmos was listening, its only response was to sandblast me with another squall. But by the end of the day, I was resting by the gently breaking waves of Portscatho, a beer in one hand and a barbecued sausage in the other. A B&B was waiting for me up the road, everything paid for by an Instagram follower, Simon Stallard, who lived nearby. We'd arranged to meet on The Path, but I had no idea that another act of generosity was coming at the time. When the news was delivered, I struggled not to choke on my food. I was laughing so hard.

Simon thumped me on the back. 'Mate, what's up with you?'

Fuck me, I thought. *It works . . . The universe has sorted me out.* Not that I was going to tell him. Simon would have thought I'd lost the plot. He then said 'the universe listens.'

The same thing happened a few days later, when having broken ground just past the Helford River. I began the long turn that would take me beyond a peninsula called The Lizard. On that occasion, I dialled up the stars and, shortly afterwards, a farmer's wife and her family – more strangers from the internet – offered me a place to stay on their nearby farm. 'We don't have a spare room,' she wrote. 'But we do have a barn.' *Well, if it's good enough for Jesus*, I thought, *then it's good enough for me.* I arrived at their cottage shortly afterwards, just in time for a simple dinner of boiled potatoes with one or two dollops of homegrown vegetables thrown in.

'It's been a tough harvest,' said the woman, looking

embarrassed at she passed the plate over. 'I'm sorry we don't have more to share.'

I wanted to hug her tightly and tell her that she'd given me more than enough. 'What are you talking about?' I said. 'Everything tastes amazing.'

I wasn't kidding. It felt like a Heston Blumenthal lunch, I was that hungry.

As we stayed up late and chatted, the hospitality of her family made my heart ache. Her two teenage boys, off from school for the summer, were desperate to remain in the conversation, even though they were due to start work on the farm at 5am. When I was eventually shown to my bed, which was a stack of hay bales in a ramshackle shed, I felt like a kid on a camping adventure. Light splashes of rain drummed at the corrugated roof as a grumbling summer storm passed by in the distance. A nervous herd of cows, my roommates for the evening, shuffled and snorted nearby. But as I settled down in my makeshift bunk, the romantic, *Boy's Own Adventure* vibe was shattered by a scratching sound that came a little too close to my ear for comfort. *A rat!* I zipped up the sleeping bag, pulled its hood tightly around my head and fell asleep, only waking when the sun came up. Stalks of straw were stuck to my face and my mouth and lips were dry and cracked. But knowing that the universe was on my side, I had the overwhelming sense that another amazing day was beginning.

* * *

I became increasingly comfortable with the concept of sofa surfing. More people approached me on Instagram with offers, recommendations and suggestions, and when I next checked my stats, I was shocked to see that I had thousands of new followers. *Shit! Maybe Tommy was on to something?* I thought, while also remembering that I didn't want to become a recognisable figure online. Even with a modest following, the problem was that these interactions – while lovely – were becoming increasingly time-consuming. I spent a small chunk of every morning writing my *hellos* and *thank yous*, while doing my best to respond to any questions about the journey, usually from people in a similar predicament to me.

Then, as moved around the Cornish shoreline and entered North Devon, another message amplified the idea that I was being powered by some mysterious momentum.

DAVID: *Hi Warrior Walker! We would love to have you over for the night. That's if you need a place to stay?*

All the altruistic gestures I'd received so far had made me far less paranoid about the risks of stranger danger, but I wasn't stupid. There was a quick social media check, and once my nerves had been settled, I confirmed that David's gesture was greatly appreciated. Shortly afterwards, I received a series of instructions that detailed how I should access their beautiful house in Braunton, a village that was positioned a couple of walking days away from the end of the South West Coast Path. I was stunned that anyone could be so kind and trusting.

'Are you sure?' I wrote.

'Of course! Just come in. We'll be back after work, around seven.'

Their house was not small and though I'd been given a direct invitation, I still felt terrible entering their home unsupervised.

Not wanting to create any awkwardness, I dropped my Bergen in the kitchen and left the house. The thought of them finding me in *their* home, on *their* sofa, eating *their* chocolate biscuits felt a little bit rude, so I decided to explore the village. My plan was to knock on their front door when they arrived later that day, while doing my best to convey a friendly vibe. As I walked, I even prepared my all-important first impression by practising a smile and a wave that hopefully said: *I'm weird. But I'm not a weirdo.*

Later, when I returned, there was still no sign of my hosts. So, rather than loitering, I played a game in which I imagined their day-to-day lives by looking up at the house for clues, like a contestant in *Through the Keyhole* – the nineties TV gameshow presented by Loyd Grossman. *So, who lives in a house like this?* A nuclear scientist? A government minister? A property tycoon? The furnishings and fittings had a Scandi-style vibe. *One of them must have lived in Sweden and been an interior designer,* I thought. *Or Norway. Or Denmark. Maybe even Finland.*

The game didn't last very long; I was all out of northern European countries. And when David and his wife Nicola arrived, there was a whirlwind of handshakes and hugs and offers of food, drinks and hot showers. All my preconceptions were shattered. They turned out to be neither Scandinavian nor design gurus. Nobody had worked in nuclear physics. Property deals and government bureaucracy weren't a feature on their CVs either. Instead, David was former army major now operating as a consultant while Nicola worked as a GP. As we sat around their kitchen, I was instantly made to feel at home, and it was decided I should stay for two nights.

'But honestly, Paul, you can stay for as long as you like,' said Nicola. 'Our home is yours.'

I smiled, trying to recall another time when I'd felt so safe and seen. Nicola and David seemed like good souls. They wanted the best for other people – I could tell by the way they spoke of their parents, siblings, and nieces and nephews. As we cleared the kitchen table of dinner plates, unbothered by the late hour, Nicola bombarded me with questions. Lots of them. She wanted to know about my home life, my motivations for joining The Path, and the realities of a world disconnected from systems and security. When it came to talking about my family, I opened my wallet and pulled out the dog-earned photo of Nan and Grandad on their boat trip in Skye.

'They're one of the reasons I'm still here,' I said, reaching into my t-shirt to show Nicola the St Christopher's locket around my neck.

'Why? What happened?' she said.

'Because nobody knew what was going on inside my mind and I was a mess,' I said, the tears welling up. 'On the outside, I was blagging it. I told everyone I was feeling great, when I wasn't. It was all a lie. Dad wasn't around to talk to and Mum didn't care. But Nan and Grandad did . . .'

I explained how my brother had been kicked out of the house at the age of 13 and if it hadn't been for our grandparents care, he'd have ended up in a home. Then, when I came to do my GCSE exams at the age of 16, Mum had disappeared to Cyprus for a two-week holiday, leaving me to fend for myself at arguably one of the most important stages in my formative life. I lived off microwave meals and pretended to everybody at school that I was OK. At my part-time job in the local supermarket, I acted as if my parents' behaviour was totally normal to anyone that mentioned it, but really, I was in a terrible state: lonely, depressed and bloody scared.

That sense of disconnection carried on into the Marines, especially during those first few weeks as I found my feet in basic training. The work often seemed insurmountable. But whenever I felt homesick, a little reminder of my dysfunctional family life usually jolted me back to reality. One afternoon, while standing on the parade ground with my fellow Marines-in-waiting, our platoon corporal singled me out in the line-up.

'Recruit Harris!' he bellowed. I could tell he wanted everybody to hear my name.

I looked up at him, fearful of what was about to happen. 'Corporal!'

'Recruit Harris, we've had some correspondence from your mum. She's called us to say that you're not to come home.'

I felt sick. The humiliation was crushing. As was the realisation that, no matter what happened to me, in times of trouble I was never going to be caught by the safety net of a loving family – not fully. Something broke inside me that day and from then on I regarded myself a failure, despite passing out through Royal Marines basic training and going on to enjoy a successful military career. Whenever I went home, during leave, I presented a façade of happiness to everyone I encountered – the classic deflection strategy. But if I was with my nan, the truth of how I was feeling always came through and I'd talk freely about how unhappy I was. Grandad sometimes had limited time for my emotional discomfort. He'd lived through the Second World War and was part of a generation of men for whom talking about feelings was taboo.

'Pull yourself together,' he'd sometimes say before leaving the room.

But Nan would step in. She understood me and wanted the best for my life. 'It's OK,' she'd say, giving me a big hug. 'We're going to work it out and everything will be fine. You'll see.'

But when she'd died around ten years later, everything fell apart.

Nicola gave me a hug. 'You don't have to talk about it if you don't want to.'

'No, it's OK,' I said, composing myself. 'I do want to. It's important.'

I took a deep breath. Then I told the story of how I'd found Nan unconscious one morning. I was in my early thirties and working nights, out of the military and unsure of what the fuck I wanted to do with my life. I'd been staying with her at the time, and having come home after a long shift, I'd known something was up almost immediately. Grandad had passed away by then and Nan was always glued to the news, usually from around 7am – I think it kept her company as she made breakfast alone. But that morning, the house was silent. I ran upstairs, panicking and shouting, and found her passed out on the bathroom floor. When she eventually came to, Nan insisted on driving herself to the doctor's, where a mini-stroke was diagnosed. A succession of tests and scans then found several tumours. *Nan's got cancer.* The words, when I heard them, sounded like they were happening to another person. The disease had spread aggressively. Her prognosis wasn't good.

Nan would need regular doses of chemo and, even then, the chances of her surviving were slim.

Retelling the story to Nicola was reopening old wounds; everything felt so raw again. I remembered back to how I'd felt during my first day on The Path, with the old lady and her dog. Another wobble was coming.

Nicola held my hand. 'It's OK, Paul.'

'I know,' I said, weakly. 'It's just so hard because I remember the bad stuff as much as the good . . .'

'Like what?'

'The chemo smell: *it was everywhere*. I'd come home from night shifts and it was like it had permeated the house. Nan was so miserable. The treatment was killing her and she felt ill and stressed, and I think she knew the end was coming. I remember we had a long chat about death one night, around Christmas time. Before the diagnosis, I'd planned to teach in Thailand in the new year, but I wanted to look after her instead. Nan wouldn't have it, though. She said that my brother could help and that I should live my life . . . So that's what I did because it's what Nan had wanted. But it was so fucking heartbreaking.

'Then she said that the time had come to end the chemo. When I asked her why, she said it was because she didn't want to be in pain anymore. I couldn't argue with that. She was living, but she wasn't alive because everything in her body was hurting so badly. The treatment was worse than the illness. I can remember the last time I hugged her, when I left to go to Thailand. She made me promise not to come home because of her. And then at the very end, when she was in hospital again and couldn't really talk, my cousin had put me on the phone so I could say goodbye. And I told her that I loved her so much—'

Nicola was squeezing my hand tightly now. 'I'm so sorry, Paul,' she said.

'We all lose loved ones,' I sniffed. 'No one gets away from that.'

'Yeah, but she would be so proud of you,' said Nicola. 'Of what you're doing.'

She pointed to the photo, now set down on the table. 'Are you going back there?'

I looked at the picture. 'To Skye? Well, I'm going past it, so I could. Maybe. *I suppose.*'

'You really should,' said Nicola. 'I think it'll help.'

I honestly hadn't thought about it before. Not because Skye was an emotional trigger point, but because I'd felt like a mess for so long and the idea of celebrating someone else's life, somewhere else, hadn't flashed on my radar. I'd been too busy dealing with mine, especially when I'd been stuck at home with Dad, as he did his best to remind me that the cornerstones of modern existence were a solid career, 2.4 children, retirement and finally death. I'd already turned my back on that, believing happiness could be found in adventure, but I also had to find a turning point if I was to heal from some of the hurt I was feeling. Maybe it *was* Skye?

When I went to bed, I took another look at the photo. Nan and Grandad were so happy back then. My dream was to look that happy at some point in the future, too.

Then I considered the *what ifs* . . .

* * *

Nicola was the boss of the house, at once kind and caring, and blunt and honest, like the best kind of sergeant major. On Sunday, the whole family were invited over to meet me, and her guestlist included her parents and a sister, plus the several nieces and nephews she'd spoken about during my first night. A massive roast dinner was served and I felt my endorphins racing. Not because the food was so good but because the human contact was so real. It had been missing in my world for such a long time that I'd forgotten it could exist. Surrounded by Nicola and David and their extended family, I realised I was living the comfort I'd once craved as a kid. Meanwhile, I had to bend to several standards and rules I hadn't experienced previously. At one point, when I was scrolling through my phone at the dinner table, Nicola gently scolded me.

'Paul, be present,' she said kindly. 'We're eating.'

She was right, and I shrank a little with embarrassment. But only because I hadn't been subjected to a home environment with a similar set of manners before. In my parents' house, nobody had cared, and the realisation made me feel a little self-conscious. Shortly after, as everyone swapped stories, I became worried that I was an inconvenience or maybe outstaying my welcome.

I asked David quietly, 'Am I in the way?'

The response was warm and reassuring. 'No, you're not,' he said. 'We think you're great.'

At the words, emotion snagged in my throat and my eyes puddled with tears.

You're so lucky to be here, I thought. *You're so lucky to be in this . . .*

When I later told them as much, Nicola gave me a squeeze. 'Look, I love what you're saying, and I love what you're about, but I'm stepping in here. You've created this . . . *your own luck*. If you hadn't stepped up and recognised the dangers you were in and started on The Path, you wouldn't be here. *You* have brought yourself to this point, no one else. Luck is a myth. I don't believe in it. The challenge for you now is to find your *enough* in life.'

I felt confused. 'What do you mean?'

'Well, everyone has a different *enough*,' continued Nicola. 'The things they need in life, rather than the stuff they want. For some people, it's a roof over their head. Maybe good health and a loving partner. That's their enough. The problem is, a lot of people confuse their *enough* with their wants, and in chasing stuff that's out of reach, they become unhappy. Paul, you need to work out what you need to be happy once this is finished. You need to figure out your *enough*.'

I sighed, knowing I'd asked the universe for this challenging moment and it had delivered – big time. My job now was to act.

CHAPTER EIGHT

FORGIVE, FORGET

I ended up staying with David and Nicola for three weeks.

Physically, I wasn't ready to move again. When I'd prepared to leave for the end of the South West Coast Path and then Wales, my feet began throbbing angrily. As I checked my kit and washed my clothes, the ligaments in my arches burned and my toes still felt numb from all the walking. Nicola, with her medical expertise and won't-take-no-for-an-answer demeanour, ordered me to sit down. Then she took off my socks for a physical examination. There was a gasp and then an awkward silence.

'Paul, there is *no way* you're walking on these,' she said, tutting at my recklessness. 'They're black and blue.'

I winced, less in pain and more with embarrassment. My toenails resembled a line of cracked tombstones. 'Yeah, OK,' I said sheepishly. 'I'll rest for a bit.'

My feet were strapped and Nicola ordered me to the sofa in

what was the politest house arrest imaginable, my step count reduced to a series of short hobbles, either to the toilet or upstairs to bed. After a couple of recovery days, I finished the last kilometres of the South West Coast Path and then rested for two weeks, embarking on one or two gentle test walks with David. Autumn was being seasonally volatile, careering between heatwaves and hurricane winds, and with every shower, the realities of a homeless winter felt painfully real. For weeks, I'd promised to only worry about the bad weather when it happened. *Now it was happening.* Though I felt physically ready, my nervous system bristled at the thought of walking for at least four months in the freezing cold.

I was also sad to leave the family connection behind – it was one I'd craved all my life. When I'd taken my first steps in July, Dad eyeballing me suspiciously, his barely disguised disappointment trailing me as I walked away from Coast Café, I'd felt emotionally hollow. Probably because the house I was living in was less a home and more an emotional storage unit packed with resentment, fear and loneliness. I didn't want to go back there. But with Nicola and David, there was nothing but love and a shared currency of respect, admiration and affection. Over the space of three weeks, we'd become bundled up in it during our walks, dinners and long chats on life, death and love. It felt cosy. They had seen me for who I truly was and I had seen their *enough*. When the day came to leave them, I felt heartbroken.

'Humans are great,' I said, burying my face into Nicola's shoulder as we hugged tightly, standing on the driveway.

'Just know you're loved here, Paul,' she said.

David joined me for my first few kilometres back on The Path. He loved walking with me, as I did with him, and there was one more wind-blasted stroll for us to enjoy. But he also had a question to ask.

'You know, I've been talking with Nicola. If you're not doing anything this Christmas, you can always come back. You know, to stay with us . . .'

He was throwing me a lifeline. A proper Christmas with a proper family. I hadn't experienced one before and the sense of belonging, of being wanted, was instantly reassuring. Here was the safety net Mum and Dad hadn't given me.

' . . . That's if you're not doing anything else? We don't want you sleeping in a bush when you could be with us.'

I couldn't think of anything better; my Christmases had always been a car wreck. While serving in the Marines, I boozed heavily during the holidays and barely communicated with Mum and Dad, or my brother or my stepbrothers. They didn't want me at their respective houses, I didn't want to be at theirs, so I made alternative arrangements because the familial environment was hardly conducive to a holiday of peace, love and goodwill to all men. In the end, I came to dread it. Later, once I'd moved to Thailand, where the holiday season wasn't celebrated, Christmas became nothing more than a weird afterthought and I happily stuck my head in the sand about it all. But a break with Nicola and David would be a totally different experience and the idea of it lifted me. I had something to get excited about. For the first time ever, there was a proper home to go to.

I bit his hand off. 'Alright,' I said.

David laughed. 'Well, take some time to think about it. We honestly won't be offended if you feel the need to stay out.'

Not a chance. My mind was made up. 'I'll be there. So make sure you've got enough gravy . . .'

When I eventually trudged away from him, feeling teary, I realised that the support of Nicola and David and their extended family was giving me something entirely unexpected. Reassurance. A sense that I was heading in the right direction. As far as they were concerned, what I was doing carried merit, it deserved recognition, and the undertaking was one I should be proud of. Rather than talking down to me about what I'd been doing wrong, or how I should be paying the bills with a monthly wage, they were lifting me up about what I was doing *right*. After three weeks in their company, I didn't feel as lost as I had done previously. Yes, the way forward was still shrouded in fog but at least I was able to feel my feet on the ground. When I looked at the map and my position towards the end of the South West Coast Path, I realised I'd travelled roughly around 1,000 kilometres. There were still thousands to go. But with the love of Nicola and David behind me that distance instantly felt a lot less daunting.

I was being propelled forward with rocket fuel.

* * *

Having rejoined The Path, I couldn't shake the feeling that I'd been given a chance to properly reassess my life. Walking, while uninterrupted by technology and people, meant I could breathe and think without distractions. *So, what is my enough?* For the next few days, Nicola's question pressed on me like a blister. It forced me to consider purpose, love and family, and it dawned on me that I had been blaming myself for the lack of care in my family home. That was understandable: a lot of kids find it hard to accept that the negative things that happen in their lives aren't necessarily about them. I was no different. Dad wasn't around when I was little. My attitude: *that must be because of something I've done*. Mum was also absent a lot of the time. My attitude: *that must be because of something I've done, too.*

Inevitably, as I'd grown older and angrier, my parents copped the blame for everything. But having experienced so much kindness during my short time on The Path, the negative emotion was dissipating. I realised Mum and Dad would have endured plenty of pain and heartache in their lives, just as I had. There was every chance they'd loved me very much when I was a little kid but they hadn't been able to express it for whatever reason. That certainly seemed the case once I'd returned home from Thailand and moved in with my dad again. I'd not seen him for seven years at that point and for as long as I'd known him, he'd been a butcher. He was living a nice, settled life in a cosy house in Bournemouth. I would have been a disruptive arrival.

It was kind of him to take me back. I knew that. But our reunion was doomed from the off, and I remember feeling as if the walls were closing in on me almost from the minute I stepped through the front door. That had nothing to do with Dad, of course. I fell into a trap familiar to a lot of adults when they spend an extended period with their folks: I reverted to the teenage version of myself. I felt misunderstood.

I struggled to grasp the emotions that were upending me – in this case, depression. Worse, I became sulky, unpredictable and downright moody. I was having a nightmare time. It can't have been a lot of fun for Dad either.

When I thought about it, I saw that this episode was the painful, inevitable conclusion to a fractured childhood with Mum and Dad, one that created a doom loop which only worsened over time. In the Marines, I turned myself into a physical savage because I couldn't talk to anyone about what I'd gone through at home. Becoming an aggressive Marine seemed like the only way to survive. My outlook on life was impacted as a result, so when people displayed kindness, I rarely trusted them. If they gave me compliments, I laughed them off or made self-deprecating comments, when a simple 'thank you' would have done. I felt unheard a lot of the time and believed, wrongly, that my opinions were unimportant.

Whenever Dad tried to communicate with me as a young adult and then after my return to the UK, I became closed off. *So how would he have known what was going on during my lowest moments?* I thought. Whenever I felt pain, or shame, I masked my feelings. *So how could he have been expected to help?* On the rare occasions when we did communicate on an emotional level, usually after I'd experienced a panic attack or meltdown, both of us fell into a series of predictable pitfalls. *So how could he have reacted appropriately?* I asked myself these questions continuously on The Path and found a simple answer: we had become stereotypes. Dad expressed his frustration at what I was doing wrong and how I should fix my issues. I became angry at his rigid values.

After leaving Nicola and David's place, my attitude was softening. I realised that meeting people who were interested in what I was doing was filling my cup up with warm emotions and I was now able to view myself through their eyes. When I'd spoken to that old lady on my first day, the act of saying hello felt unnatural and mechanical. It was something I had to force, rather than deliver on instinct. Soon, the greetings and chats became second nature, and I buzzed off the dopamine that accompanied every new meeting. While there was no doubt I still felt emotionally exposed whenever I retold my story, the reaction of others helped me to accept a different perspective. I was becoming increasingly untethered from my past life. The misfortunes looked different; my survival was something to be proud of. And rather than viewing the heartbreaks as a litany of bad luck stories that had happened *to* me – and were therefore something uncontrollable and shameful – I saw them as being lived *by* me. This one shift in perspective reclaimed a little power from the darkest moments and my emotional wounds transformed into defining battle scars. I wasn't yet healed or in an ideal mental state, but I was optimistic about my future for the first time in ages. *Maybe the fixing process is starting?* I thought, hopefully.

Then a warm feeling grew in my chest.

'I forgive you, Dad,' I said out loud one morning. 'All the pain and hurt and everything you've given me, and all the unanswered questions that I have . . . I'm going to say: *it's OK*.'

And then I walked on.

* * *

I might have been starting to feel more emotionally at peace, but now I was back to being physically exposed on The Path, not knowing where I'd sleep next or when I'd wash, my daily stresses returned. The early-morning sea dips of July and August were abandoned, given the cold temperatures, but I was able to maintain a good walking pace, soon leaving Minehead – the finishing point of the South West Coast Path – and then passing through Weston-super-Mare and Portishead. I celebrated by pushing on to Wales as quickly as I could and enjoyed the symbolic moment of crossing over the Severn Bridge and into *a different bloody country* by taking a detour to find a coffee shop in nearby Chepstow. I wanted to savour the moment.

BAM! The sensory overload of voices, barking dogs and clattering plates rocked me from the serenity of the past few weeks. Surrounded by noise and human traffic, I instantly felt like a totally different person, at odds with the pace of life around me. The frothing, grinding and steaming machines sounded more like a building site full of drills, jackhammers and chugging steamrollers. Rattled, I later stomped towards Newport, where the everyday hustle and bustle of townie life smashed into me like a tsunami. I hadn't seen as many people in one place for the best part of a year.

During my last few months in Bournemouth, lockdown had sealed me off from civilisation, like everyone else. The Path had been almost deserted and the last time I'd stepped through a cityscape was Exeter, which had been fairly empty given the social distancing restrictions in place. Newport was a different vibe. Its frantic energy felt dizzying and I was reminded of those discombobulating days when I'd return to England, after long periods away in Iraq and Afghanistan when the bleeping crossings, rain-spattered traffic and fast-moving normality felt like a fairground ride. I'd want to get off. My chest would tighten; my head jangled with the stress. But a couple of days later, my body and brain would usually acclimatise to the stimulus, so I knew how to readjust in Newport. I walked and walked until the buzzing in my brain quietened and my breathing slowed to a steady rate.

But everything was so different in Wales. The voices. The atmosphere. The street signs. It was a shock to the system, and for a moment, the negative voices came rushing back, louder than ever before.

Why are you doing this?

What will you do when your money runs out?

How will you cope when the weather turns bad?

I silenced them with some warming reminders of who I was and what I was doing. There was Nicola and David's Christmas dinner to look forward to. I'd completed the South West Coast Path and stepped into Wales. And when I checked my social media accounts, there were more offers of beds, barns and bothies. They peppered the route ahead like homing beacons and I used each one as a motivational power-up. I then learned that someone had created a tracker of my progress – a website that followers could use to trace my footsteps as I walked. Staring at it in disbelief, I contacted the designer, who introduced himself as Brad and told me he'd been through a rough patch. At one point, he'd thought about ending his life. With the help of his wife and family, Brad had pulled himself through.

'I wish I was doing what you are,' he said, obviously unaware of the pain of walking daily marathons. 'I couldn't give you any money in support, but I could design a website. So, I did . . .'

His work had attracted a small army of followers. Among them, a class of nine-year-olds from Saint Gabriel's Catholic School in Newport. For the past few weeks, the kids and their teacher had apparently been tracking my progress, using my route as an educational resource. Having noticed that I was passing nearby, they asked if I'd like to come in and say hello. Pushing aside the trauma of singing 'Ba Ba Black Sheep' to a classroom of Thai kids, I showed up, plonked myself on a stool in the assembly hall and answered a flood of questions:

Where have you been?

What's your favourite dog?

What's the weirdest place you've been to the toilet?

The boys wanted to know about my time in the military; the girls wanted to know why I read paper maps rather than digital ones. Once my talk had concluded, the school's priest offered to bless me. I thought back to the priest at Exeter Cathedral and smiled. *Why not?* It was keeping with the vibe. Then one of the pupils gave me a card. When I opened it, a cheque for £100 had been folded inside.

'That should get you some more coffees and cakes on the walk,' said the priest.

I didn't know what to say.

It was to get even lovelier. Every military person of a certain age will have heard of the Falklands War veteran Simon Weston – a former British soldier who was horrifically burned when the ship he was travelling on came under attack from Argentine

Skyhawk fighter planes. The stories of his awful injuries made national headlines, as had his reconstructive surgery. Simon was a warning to every solider of just how brutal war could be. When Instagram announced him as my latest follower, I froze in shock. Then I dropped into his messages to say hello.

@warriorwalker: Would be an honour to buy you a coffee.

@simonweston: If we can sort it, I'm good for a coffee.

We arranged to meet in a Cardiff café, where we chatted for hours. Me, about my story, The Path and the kindness of strangers. Him, about survivor's guilt, faith and imposter syndrome. The meeting blew my mind. People outside of my immediate orbit, *famous people,* were being drawn to my challenge in ways that I hadn't expected. For the first time on my journey, I connected with a sense of purpose. The Path suddenly felt so much bigger than me. All I had to do was finish it.

All this unexpected attention meant that another level of pressure had been added. *I really don't want to let anyone down,* I thought, as I moved around the Welsh coast, the temperatures dropping, the rains stampeding in and the walking becoming considerably tougher.

Then 2020 took another weird twist, as rumours of a forthcoming 'mini lockdown' ricocheted around the coffee shops and beachside benches. I didn't care. I was in the swing of things, making good progress along the coast, walking steadily until 19 December, when I marked my location and turned around for Nicola and David's, my momentum super-charged by the thought of several days celebrating with people who loved me and who I loved, and my first ever proper Christmas celebration. I walked back to Llanelli and caught a train to their house. I stepped through the front door and hugged the family, my Bergen hitting the floor. I took in the decorations, the tree and the intoxicating togetherness of it all. The six o'clock news was echoing through the hallway, but a depressingly familiar story was being played on repeat:

Covid numbers are rocketing.

The hospitals can't cope.

Increased restrictions will stem the tide of infections and help the NHS.

The mini lockdown had been agreed. *So, what the fuck do I do now?* I thought. Returning to my spot on the map on 28 December as I had planned suddenly felt unworkable.

Nicola seemed to read my mind. 'Make this place your home,' she said. 'You can live here for as long as it takes.'

I ended up staying for three months.

CHAPTER NINE

THE WHISPERINGS OF THE PATH

My memories of that wintery lockdown are now patchy. I know it went on forever, what with several circuit breaker extensions as Groundhog Day became Groundhog Weeks became Groundhog Months. Only my daily walks worked as a brief flight to nature and the wider world. All of us were Zoomed out. And everywhere I looked, the dramatic skies of the South West Coast Path provided an ethereal reminder of some lost snapshot of humanity: an optimistic sunrise, all pinging beams of reflective watery light; a brooding wintery sunset with its spreading bruise of purples and oranges. While beautiful, these moments were discordant, especially without the company of other people, like a famous guitar riff played out of tune. Every day, the three of us made assurances to one another. *At some point in the future, we'll share these sunsets with mates . . .*

in an actual pub garden. Or: *Can you imagine what it's going to be like to hug a stranger at the football or a festival?* The last vapours of a destructive pandemic were taking forever to disappear. Fantasising about normality seemed like the only way forward.

I could only hang out at David and Nicola's for so long. I'd loved to have stayed forever, and they were more than happy to host me, but it was important I regained some form of independence. The whole point of joining The Path in the first place had been to wrestle back control of my rudderless life. I wanted to move forward, especially as a real sense of purpose had been building in Wales, and surrendering my challenge to a period of comfort and care, while bloody amazing, was beginning to feel like a cop out.

When Simon – who I'd connected with in Portscatho and who had been generous enough to get me a room in a B&B – called and mentioned he needed help at his Hidden Hut beach restaurant in Porthcurnick, I put myself forward. We sorted out some accommodation in Portscatho and it was agreed I would be looked after in return for food and cash as I worked the spring and summer season. I needed some money for my next walking stint, and earning a regular paycheque made me feel less of a burden and more of a self-sufficient human. When the moment came, I told myself, I would join The Path again.

The long shifts making pizzas and serving coffees gave me time to reflect on everything that had happened so far. Physically, the effort had proved a lot harder than initially expected. When I'd taken my first steps, the plan was to nail a daily marathon, a yomp of 40-plus kilometres, which seemed like a realistic target.

I was young enough to cope with the grind, trained to endure physical discomfort and emotionally prepared for anything the elements might chuck at me. I was also desperate enough to succeed. What I hadn't considered was the brutal terrain: the endless climbs; sandy beaches that seemed to drag me down to the waterline; precarious scrambles over seaweed-splattered boulders. On some days, I rolled over in my sleeping bag and ached from a night spent snoring in a hedge. When the offers of beds and barns first came through, I had felt guilty at accepting the hospitality. *Am I a fraud?* I thought. Then I realised that the support was part of the story, like an energy gel in an ultramarathon, and I'd be stupid not to accept it.

In that respect, I'd started to care less about the opinions of others. The imposter syndrome that Simon Weston had spoken of over coffee – a man whose bravery stood unquestioned – was a universal hangup, not unique to me. It came for everyone. In the first few months of walking, Stroudy had mentioned that several critical voices were echoing across social media about my adventure. Some of them were peers from the Marines; they sneered at my claims I would walk non-stop for days on end and used online platforms to take the piss. Some of the criticism was valid. *Yeah, it's not exactly Everest, is it?* But it was *my* Everest. A challenge I'd undertaken to turn my life around. While their attitude stung at first, my progress along the map showed me I was making good on my promise, and on my terms. *So, fuck them*, I thought. *Be proud of yourself.*

There had been so much fear when I'd first stepped outside Dad's front door. Some of that was because I didn't have a tent. I couldn't afford one and the kit in my bag was either old or borrowed. During the summer, I'd worried about what might happen if I was exposed to the elements for too long, especially in a storm or gale, and cut off from civilisation. I'd stressed even more about what might happen in the winter when hypothermia was a very real risk, especially the further north I travelled. But I'd also been concerned about the reaction of anyone passing by. Technically, I was homeless and wandering the coastal trails during a time when most people were being encouraged to stay indoors and away from others. I hadn't been sure if my presence would draw a negative reaction. Everything felt like a massive leap of faith.

But those fears were unfounded. I'd experienced nothing in the way of hostility or suspicion. Nobody had called me out for taking my journey, even though technically I should have sometimes only been outside for an hour or two a day. And nobody called the police. If anything, I experienced the complete opposite. Kindness showed up wherever I went, as evidenced by those spare rooms and hotels. Whenever I felt like I was approaching a moment of desperation, either through being knackered or concerned about my sleeping arrangements, somebody came through to help.

Partly that was down to my attitude. I'd decided to walk without headphones a lot of the time, and by forcing myself to chat to the people I passed, I became more open and expressive. *Hi, how are you?* Those four words became a gateway and the response to my story, whenever someone asked to hear it, was usually supportive. People offered encouragement or advice. They introduced me to their dogs and friends. And they passed on my story to people further along The Path. By the time I arrived in the next town or village, someone was usually looking out for me, hoping to talk about what I'd been doing or wanting to help.

I learned that the best coffees were those drunk from a heavy mug with an interested stranger, especially if they had a scruffy dog with them. As an espresso machine chuntered in the background, it felt so good to fall in and out of conversation with a random – someone I might have met outside on the beach or a person who'd noticed of me while settling down at a table. The Bergen was an ice breaker. The regulars in coffee shops and shacks on the beaches of Cornwall, Dorset and Devon were used to hikers taking on the coastal path, but generally, none of them carried a backpack loaded down with year-long supplies. Despite Stroudy's ruthless edit, mine was still stacked with redundant equipment and people wondered aloud whether I was living on The Path rather than exploring it. When I answered that, yes, I was officially homeless, their ears pricked up. When they then wanted to know what I intended to do, having finished the South West Coast Path, the answer often threw them into a loop. *I'm going to walk the rest of Britain.* A lot of people wanted to know whether I fancied a beer rather than a coffee. But a hot drink with a stranger was everything I needed because it brimmed with optimism and potential. The last coffee was always my favourite. The coffee I was most excited by was the next; the most satisfying coffee existed in the now.

These meetings were changing me dramatically and for the better. Whenever I talked to someone – about my life and theirs – I felt a lightness, and the aches and pains in my back and shoulders faded away, as if I'd been plugged into the mains.

As a kid, I'd known it was good to talk, but the opportunity had rarely presented itself. As a grown adult, I understood the importance of being open about any struggles I might have been facing, but the doing felt so hard, especially as the environment I was accustomed to had hardly been conducive to an honest and vulnerable conversation about *me* – not at home, not at work and certainly not on reality TV. I feared the opinions of others; insecurity dangled from my neck like a noose, and I worried that any negative comments from my friends, family or peers would hang me with it. I hated crying too because I'd been taught by the military that sensitivity was a sign of weakness rather than a strength. But on The Path, I could talk about my hurt to another person. That person listened. And I felt better.

It was showing too. When setting off in 2020, my back had been hunched, my shoulders weighed down by the mental heft of everything I'd gone through, as well as the small house strapped to my body. The sense of purpose I'd experienced in Newport also became amplified because it was creating a feedback loop online. More people, lots of them men, checked in to tell me they'd found themselves in a similar situation, especially after some massive life upheaval. Unable to ask for help, they became suffocated by depression and anxiety until a depressingly familiar question appeared: *What's the bloody point?* Some of them had been able to find an escape route away from the wreckage. They were eager to share their stories. Others were still a work in progress. They wanted to know more about what I'd been through and what I thought was a sensible step forward. For each one, I explained I was nowhere near to being over the darkness. 'I don't know myself,' I'd say. 'I'm just trying to be different.' But I wondered: was The Path a substitute for therapy? *Because sometimes it felt that way.*

People got in touch to talk about my favourite parts of the walk so far. Others wanted to know how they could do something similar. Everyone was so sick to the back teeth of staying indoors, while feeling cowed by an invisible illness, that the thought of walking away from their front door and into a fantastical escape, even in the pissing rain, seemed seductive, daring and outrageous. Like something out of a Paulo Coelho novel. Local newspapers called my number for interviews. The BBC wanted to run a piece on me, Sky too. I felt validated but also fraudulent, because these requests, while exciting, landed with me as I made coffees and served pizzas. The Path snaked by the bar outside, around the flattened sands and gently crashing waves. If I wanted, I could touch it or walk along it in bare feet. But it felt a million miles away because Simon was busy with work, business was good, and I really didn't want to let him down by quitting.

But I didn't want to let myself down either.

Every day, The Path whispered at me. I tried to ignore it but I couldn't because it was relentless. It knew that I was masking the truth about where I was and what I was doing. Yes, I was glad for the security and happy to add to my meagre cash reserves so that I could be less cautious about my daily spending once the walking started again. But as I worked into the summer of 2021, I felt the heat of the sun, the calming rhythms of the tide and the briny tang of the sea. Passing walkers mentioned what they'd seen around the trail; some of them knew me from my Instagram page and asked why I wasn't further along the track. Every mention of the journey made me realise what I was missing. I had to get moving again.

In the end, I realised what was holding me back was a weird sense of anxiety about my physical state. By autumn, I'd been living a relative life of luxury for close to nine months, working my arse off all day and drinking at the weekend. While I wasn't out of shape, I wasn't match fit either, and the thought of hoisting my Bergen and yomping for several thousand kilometres gave me the shivers. When I looked at the pinned position on the map – Llanelli, my last spot on The Path before I'd packed up for Nicola and David's – I realised I still had so far to walk. But the pull was unmistakable. At times, it was as if the tide was dragging me closer, hoping to magnetise me to the coast so that it could slingshot me northwards. I had dreams where I was trekking around some idyllic stretch of coastline, the water surging around me, a low-lying sunset marking the end goal. When I woke, there was always a brief sense of happiness. And then a massive downer as reality kicked in. *The Path wasn't happening today. I had to go to work.*

In the end, I couldn't take it anymore. In October 2021, I handed in my notice, packed up my Bergen and stepped onto The Path for the first time in nearly ten months.

At first, my body was furious. By the time I'd arrived in Llanelli, via a couple of short walks and a train, everything ached again. *No change there then,* I thought. My muscles weren't yet prepared for the effort to come and everything was a baptism of fire. Then, as I walked from Llanelli to Pembroke and around to St Davids, the weather turned miserable.

It rained nearly every day, in heavy rods, during one of the wettest months I'd experienced. Water dripped from my nose and pooled in the edges of my hood, soaking my neck and snail-trailing down my back and chest. My bones felt damp. My toes ached endlessly. When I looked at the sea, it churned wildly, the slate grey deep topped with a frothing white, the wind driving an icy spray inland towards anyone stupid enough to stand at the water's edge.

There were times when I wondered if the universe had become angry with me. I worried that the connection I'd forged with nature, a union first triggered by joining with The Path, was now severed, due to my time away. I told myself that this was yet another test, a challenge to see how much I wanted the healing prize at the end, and I should work even harder to win back the support built during those first few months when I'd spoken to the stars and seen the stag.

I pulled my backstraps tighter and walked into the squall.

CHAPTER TEN

REMEMBER YOU WILL DIE

The idea of a support wagon hadn't crossed my mind before. And yet, there I was, sitting in a VW Transporter alongside the driver, Gareth, a muscular bloke with dark brown hair and a beard. With a day bag on my lap, a homemade packed lunch of sandwiches, fruit and snacks stuffed inside, I stared nervously at the rain hammering at the road ahead. It struck the roof with a percussive rhythm and sloshed around the squeaking windscreen wipers. The heater was working overtime, but my breath still fogged in the morning air. I was bloody freezing.

Gareth pulled up to the coastal trail. It looked muddy. 'You ready?' he said, probably wanting to get on with his day.

No, I thought. 'Yes,' I lied, zipping up my jacket, stepping out and immediately soaking my foot in an unseen puddle. My toes shrivelled.

The idea of having a temporary support car that collected

me from a nightly finishing point and then dropped me at the same spot the following morning, all tracked by GPS, had first been suggested by Gareth, an increasingly frequent voice on my Instagram feed. A professional sailor with an adventurous streak, he lived in Dale, a picturesque seaside village on the Pembrokeshire coast, known for its smattering of beach-facing houses, most of them painted in bright blue, pastel pink and Lego brick orange. This was an off-the-beaten-track holiday destination, unspoiled by influencers and YouTubers, and it looked amazing. When Gareth later invited me to stay, he explained how his mum ran a guest house near the seafront. 'She'd love to put you up,' he said. 'Mum's used to dealing with strangers.' It sounded perfect.

When I arrived, the building was gorgeous, a five-bedroom Georgian home framed with wooden beams and slanting ceilings. A large ship's anchor flaked and rusted in the front garden. Gareth had already explained how his family tree was weighed down with wanderers and trailblazers, among them his grandfather, who was famous for being one of the first explorers on Skomer – an island located a kilometre and a half off the nearby Deadman's Bay and regarded for its puffin, guillemot and razorbill communities. Gareth was now following in his grandad's footsteps, having recently rowed the Atlantic with one of his good friends. He'd been excited to swap stories and dramatic tales during our chats. *I'm going to fit in just fine*, I thought.

I was introduced to another, equally restless spirit when Gareth's mum, Ann, met me at the door. After a hug, I was told how she rarely managed more than three or four hours' kip a night after recently experiencing a tough life event. 'But you're not to feel awkward about going to bed whenever you want,' she said, ushering me in and taking my coat, before plumping every cushion in sight. 'While you're under this roof, it's your home too.'

Before long, Gareth and Katie, his partner, had arrived and I was given a guided tour of the house and sat down for dinner. Everyone was in tune with my unusual life; they understood my *why* and *how* because the family operated on similar frequency to me. That's when Gareth suggested his idea of a support car, a ride that acted like one of the motorbike couriers that buzzed around the Tour de France peloton, but without the performance-enhancing drugs.

'You'll still be walking the same distance,' he explained. 'But you'll get to rest here afterwards.'

Sounds good, I thought. 'Let's do it.'

For eight days, our car left Dale at 7am, Gareth's drive becoming progressively longer the further I walked. At 7pm, he scooped me up on the side of the trail, no matter where I was, before making an even longer journey back home. Towards the end, Gareth was driving for two hours a day. When I then crashed at the house, exhausted, unable to keep my eyes open, Ann washed my clothes and made sure that everything was fresh for the morning. As far as I was concerned, this wasn't a cheat code or a cop out, it was a supplement, like a protein shake or a sports massage, in place to help me recover and perform effectively the next day. Every morning during our ride, Gareth and I talked. When the subject of my family life came up, I made a point of saying how wonderful his mum was.

Gareth smiled. 'Thanks. I don't tell her that enough.'

'You should, bro. Take it from someone who wasn't lucky enough to have that kind of parent.'

The following day, I heard Gareth talking to Ann in the kitchen. 'Thanks for being a great mum,' he said, and I felt myself glow with pride.

In the evenings, I was left to my own devices. Some nights, the fatigue was too heavy and I struggled to recall the day in any great detail. *I walked. Got wet. Ached all over.* Then I'd shower, fall into bed and snore away a 50-kilometre yomp. On other evenings, a second wind came in and I chatted to Ann for hours, trying my best to answer her questions – and there were lots of them.

Why are you doing this? I gave her the biography.

Is there anyone special in your life? No. There was. But hopefully someone else will come along soon.

Are you running away from anything? No. I'm running *towards* something.

At the last answer, Ann looked at me weirdly. 'Like what, exactly?'

'Death,' I said, not joking.

Her eyebrows arched. 'Death? What are you talking about?'

I laughed. 'But it's a good thing. Honest, Ann.'

'OK . . . ?'

I noticed Ann had said *OK* like it was a question. 'So, how's dying a positive, then?'

'Well, it's coming for all of us, isn't it?' I said. 'At one point or another. No one's outrunning it.'

'I suppose. That's one way of looking at it . . .'

'Don't worry, I know that life's amazing, but I'm also not

scared of it ending either. We're all so comfortable with existing these days that we rarely talk about the finish, even though it's so monumental. It's coming, right? *The end*. But we don't know when that moment will be. So why not be open about it? I've seen a lot of death in my life and I've met too many people who have experienced close calls with it. I even thought about taking my own life for a while, but coming on this walk . . . I'm now appreciating the little things more and more.'

I gestured to the empty plates on the table, the smudges of a shepherd's pie on the cutlery. 'Like that dinner. Our coffees in the morning. Or the pissing wet rain blowing in off the sea. It feels awesome. *Comforting*. It inspires me. I'm thankful for it all. But that's because I've accepted these things as being finite, and I didn't think like that before. I breezed past everything, believing it would never end. Like my time in Thailand. But accepting that nothing lasts for ever means that I can enjoy everything more and feel so much happier about it.'

Ann wasn't buying it. Why would she? It was a very morbid vibe. 'It's a depressing topic, if you ask me,' she said eventually.

'If you'd met me 18 months ago, I'd have thought the same as you. No way would I have been able to have this conversation. I was a closed book. Broken. I knew I wasn't OK, so when I started The Path last year, it was partly because I wanted to figure out why.'

'And have you?' Ann began clearing away the table.

'Sort of. I was definitely overlooking the little things because I thought they'd always be there. Thinking about death, facing mine, has changed all that. I got inspired by the moment. I started hugging people for longer—'

'You'll get a reputation.'

I laughed. 'Not like that! I just love meeting people, and dogs, on the trail. It's a gift. Now I appreciate the stuff that costs nothing. And it's stopped me from thinking that I'd maybe missed the boat in some way.'

Ann laughed kindly. 'You've not missed the boat, Paul. There's a whole life ahead of you.'

Maybe. I told her I worried about money sometimes. That I was unsure of whether the special someone she'd asked about was really in my future. And how the idea of having a family of my own was a dream I clung onto, even though it might never happen. For a while, those anxieties had kept me up at night. Now they were fading into the background because I understood what it felt like to have purpose again. My encounters in South Wales with Simon Weston and the kids at Saint Gabriel's Catholic School had shown me there was an exciting world out there and I was now exploring it. I loved walking, I loved being outside, I loved people – all the little things.

I gave Ann a hug goodnight. 'I hope you're right and there's a whole life ahead of me,' I said, finally, yawning. 'But if there isn't, I'll be all right. I've got *enough*.'

* * *

After another Christmas break at Nicola and David's, I kept on walking through January 2022, knocking down the kilometres like dominoes. With the help of Gareth's support car and Ann's packed lunches, I marched along the Pembrokeshire coastline, pushing through the sideways rain past Porthgain, Fishguard and Newport, to Cardigan, Aberporth and Aberystwyth. When Gareth's VW Transporter pulled away for the last time, I walked quickly towards Tremadog and Caernarfon bays and along the dangly, rocky limb of the Llŷn Peninsula to Bangor, Llandudno and Rhyl. The progress was disorientating at times. I wondered if part of me had believed I'd actually make it this far. Because whenever I looked at my position on the coastline, I experienced a psychological form of altitude sickness.

I'm so far up the country.

Everything, and everyone I knew, was miles away and the feat seemed abstract, like experiencing a moment of hyper-awareness on a jumbo jet, thousands of metres in the air, the realisation that a steel tube weighing hundreds of tonnes was, through some feat of aeronautical engineering, soaring above the clouds. I became disorientated. There was even a change in vibe when people asked me what I was doing. While walking the South West Coast Path, I was considered a local and there was a familiarity to what I was doing. But whenever I mentioned my plan to anyone around the northernmost point of Wales, they looked at me oddly, and pulled out their phones to scroll through a map of Britain and its most westerly points. Suddenly, I was an outsider and alien.

That made me a novelty. My progress was a talking point and on some days, I had the choice of two or three households to stay with for the night, though this hospitality created several seductive pitfalls. Sometimes, after chatting with a stranger on The Path, I'd realise that an hour had passed and I was way off schedule. Then, having arrived at a host's front door, I'd see that a massive roast dinner had been prepared. Not wanting to cause offence, I'd wolf down as much as I could before drooping into a food coma and passing out on the nearest sofa or chair. But these were great problems to have and I learned to navigate them with diplomacy. Whenever a full breakfast was offered, I'd pat my belly and decline, explaining how a tummy full of bacon, sausage and eggs was a knockout gut punch that made me lethargic. (Once or twice, I puked on the trail after overeating.) With each altruistic act, I smiled at the irony of my situation. The Path had begun with a sense of familial detachment and I'd ached for some semblance of a home life. After walking along the left-hand side of the map, I'd been introduced to over 50 adoptive mums and dads.

A weird sense of tunnel vision kicked in. I was fixated on finishing my first full country and I walked for upwards of 15 hours a day, rising at 5am to hit The Path, not crashing until ten in the evening, and the workload was causing a physical toll. I was shocked by my changing physique. The weight was falling off me – some of it physical, a lot of it emotional – and my leap of faith, borne out of desperation, was paying off. On the good days, I imagined myself as a pioneer, someone breaking new ground, like a trailblazing athlete who caused rivals and fans to consider their sport in a different way. I fantasised about being the figurehead for some new walking movement – a spokesperson for the transformative benefits of living outdoors. I still knew that taking a walk in nature wasn't a silver bullet. It couldn't cure physical ailments or instantly magic away the pain of grief and depression. But it definitely helped. When someone asked what success might feel like once my walk was done, I told them: peace of mind. Because was there anything better?

Re-entry to England came via Chester. I crossed the Afon Dyfrdwy River and wandered along a bike trail towards the 'Welcome to Chester' sign, an official landmark that confirmed I'd crossed the border and finished my first full country. I buzzed at reaching such a monumental milestone. Then, a middle-aged man on a bicycle wearing hi-vis and Lycra screeched to a halt ahead of me.

'You're that Warrior Walker fella, aren't you?' he said, dismounting and shaking my hand. 'I've been following you since Land's End.'

'Really?'

'Yeah. Some journey, that.'

He introduced himself as a local policeman, reached into his pocket and shoved a tenner at me. I tingled with gratitude and spent the lot in the nearest café, while pondering what was becoming a noticeable life shift. Getting recognised was now a *thing* and I wasn't sure how I felt about it. After all, walking had been my escape route from a very dangerous situation, not a lunge for fame or attention. *Did I really want to be an influencer?* I reassured myself that getting noticed by strangers was far preferable to feeling cut off from the world, especially as I'd yomped the entire Welsh coastline. I had something tangible to take pride in; I was doing OK; I was walking taller. And the bloke looking back at me in the mirror had become likeable again. So, if people in the street wanted to say hello, or take photographs for their social media, I was open to all of it.

To go fast I had to go alone. But to go far I had to rely on the support of others.

CHAPTER ELEVEN

CHOICES

Flashback: me, sitting in Dad's kitchen. A map of Britain unfolded on a table. A notepad with a list scribbled in biro. *Places to Visit . . .*

From the minute I'd committed to walking The Path, there were parts of Britain I'd hoped to explore. One of them was the South West Coast Path, and for obvious reasons: it extended beyond my front door and around a large chunk of the country in a series of dramatic headlands and sweeping beaches. Another was the North Coast 500 (or NC500), which, as the name suggested, was an approximately 500-mile (830-kilometre) loop that tracked the northern coast of Scotland, with one or two stretches that took the walker inland. Two other regions were the Lake District and the West Highland Way, both cinematic expanses of mist-covered hills and vast waterscapes, that, despite their popularity with the thousands of tourists who visit every year, were known to bring peaceful vibes and a swaddling sense of isolation, particularly in the winter, when the weather could glitch between the breathtaking and the apocalyptic. Connections on social media suggested I veer towards the still waters at Keswick or the vertiginous inclines and rushing waterfalls near Hardknott Pass. Apparently, I'd be mad to skip past Loch Lomond and Fort William.

A couple of years on from that homely planning session, both places were getting ever nearer on The Path and I was tempted to walk them.

When am I going to get the chance again? I thought.

But visiting the Lake District and the West Highland Way presented me with a dilemma. For so long I'd hugged the shoreline, ignoring the urge to wander too far inland; on the occasions when I had ventured in-country, it was only ever for a day trip. I'd then return to my place on the coast and continue walking, having knackered myself out during the excursion. In Chester, I took a few days to sightsee the city, visiting its beautiful cathedral during a candlelit event. There were songs and prayers, and I felt at peace with myself, but I was shattered afterwards. Mainly, these trips were rare and I stayed disciplined, but it was tough because every time I looked at the map, all sorts of notable locations popped up. In Wales, the Snowdonia National Park was so close. I could see it in the distance but I stayed on target. For a while, I quite fancied going to Manchester but I carried on up the coast towards Southport instead. To yomp away from the churning sea for several weeks felt like cheating.

I was equally anxious about not having the water on my left-hand side. It had been a constant companion for thousands of kilometres; I'd grown familiar with its moods, sounds and rhythms. Whenever the whitecaps and seagulls dropped briefly out of view – if I'd walked behind a large sandbank, or stepped into a dip in the terrain – knowing they were around the next corner brought comfort. But taking a diversion inland meant jettisoning the psychological safety net and changing my stated route. Then I remembered the critics that had dismissed my challenge by comparing it to other, more dangerous missions. *What would they make of my changing plans?* I thought. Slowly, I came to the decision that I shouldn't worry about what anyone else thought about the route.

I'm just doing my thing, I told myself.

I remembered the brief. *To change my life and to save my life.*

Finally, I checked the moral compass that had kept me on track so far. The answer came back: *There is no wrong way and there is no getting lost. You're just going a different route.*

It seemed like a pretty good metaphor for life.

At Preston, I hung a right and strode inland in a north westerly direction towards the Lakes, feeling comfortable with my choices and hoping to be there in a day or so. I'd already made it further than most people had imagined and the achievement was becoming a badge of honour. I swaggered forward, my steps looser, my Bergen lighter, my confidence soaring. I was safe and looking after myself. The money I'd earned through the previous summer had given me some budgetary wiggle room, so I put it to good use by purchasing a two-man tent from a camping shop, knowing that in the event of a gale or snowstorm, I'd be OK.

At first, I rarely used it. My growing support network showed up with daily offers of rooms, caravans and even sheds. The gratitude I felt having received so much generosity from others had helped me to shrug off the paranoia of my younger self but I knew not to become complacent. Humans still unnerved me more than Mother Nature and the concept of staying in a random stranger's home always felt weird at first, no matter how often I did it or how altruistic the host's intentions were. I performed the prudent and necessary social media checks on my temporary housemates, and developed a pretty good radar on who was OK and who wasn't. But the process wasn't bombproof. Every now and then, the person I was staying with might suddenly became guarded or express nerves of their own, and I'd always put their minds at ease by explaining that I was probably more worried about them than they were about me. Thankfully, these events were generally outliers and 99 per cent of the people I stayed with were genuine, kind and eager to help. The other 1 per cent were innocuous and manageable, and during the rare close calls, I was able to extract myself without too much drama.

One night, I was invited to stay in a woman's spare bedroom for a few days and as I drifted off to sleep, the phone buzzed. It was a text from my host. She was outside my door.

I'm fighting all my feelings to come in and see you.

I felt a shiver of embarrassment and wrote back, *Don't.*

The following morning, after making my excuses and moving on, I realised that, yeah, while there was a certain naivety in what I was doing, to survive The Path, I had to grow comfortable in uncomfortable situations. I also appreciated that the dangers were considerably diminished because I was a bloke. But from then on, I made a point to only stay with couples, families and older people. Whenever an offer came through from a single woman, I'd thank them for their generosity and decline. Besides, I was knackered most of the time with barely enough energy to take off my trail shoes. Hooking up with a stranger was the last thing on my mind.

Another support wagon was established through the Lake District thanks to Chloe, as I walked a series of marathons, past the scenic towns of Kendal, Ambleside and Keswick, on towards Scotland, via a long road that took me closer to Carlisle and the border. Every morning, I packed a small bag of essentials for the day – some waterproofs, food and water – and set out as early as I could. Feeling motivated by the progress being made and the beautiful scenery, I mixed up my walks with a series of hardcore runs, thrashing myself so hard that I sometimes puked at the side of the road. I had a new mantra: *the hard work I do today will help me tomorrow*. I used it to drive me on. A man on a mission, following his own path.

* * *

I entered Scotland at Gretna Green, scene of countless ill-advised weddings, with a plan to walk through Glasgow and join the West Highland Way in Milngavie, which snaked further northwards. I was fighting fit, and my legs and back were strong, but despite entering a new country, which ordinarily would have been something to celebrate, I experienced a creeping sense of dread. Scotland was likely to be an extreme challenge, harder than anything I'd experienced previously, and while it was early spring, I stressed about the remote nature of the trails ahead. In the NC500's more remote areas, I'd probably not encounter another walker for days. *What if something happened?* The thought of breaking an ankle, or running out of food and water, and not being able to find anyone for help gave me the fear.

I pushed these shivers to the back of my mind and broke down my overall challenge into smaller, more straightforward tasks. *Put one foot in front of the other*, I told myself. *You'll be OK.*

The fear, I reckoned, could also be used to stave off any complacency going forward, but it would take a whole lot of effort to manage the stress I was now heaping upon myself. When I'd made it around Wales, the overall aim to complete my circuit of Great Britain became very real. People congratulated me on social media. Mates texted me to say well done. The general view that my walk had been nothing more than a pipe dream, and would eventually come crashing down, had been transformed into something else entirely. *Expectation.* Suddenly there was pressure and I mistakenly believed that to succeed, and to be somebody, I had to finish the lap. Anything else would be viewed as a disaster.

This idea was magnified in Glasgow. The original plan had been to enjoy the city for a few days and I even treated myself to a hotel so I could regroup before approaching the West Highland Way. But after checking in, I experienced another weird attack of situational vertigo, only this time it was more intense. *I am so far away from home,* I thought, realising that the last time I'd been this far north was during a training exercise with the Marines. Back then I'd been part of a massive collective. Twenty years on, I was very alone and feeling very exposed. Meanwhile, the big city energy outside my window was pulsing ominously. There were revving motorbikes, a jumble of traffic, and blaring police sirens. Other than a day or two in Newport, Chester and Liverpool, I'd lived a two-year rural existence, comprising barely-there coastal paths, rocky trails and extended periods of solitude. Glasgow was a whole other vibe – and it hurt.

I don't belong here, I thought. *I don't feel like myself.*

I wanted to scream into my pillow. There was a dark realisation that I was somewhere entirely alien, so, hoping to touch familiarity in the overwhelm, I looked at a city map.

Result, I thought. The nearest coffee shop was about five minutes away.

Then I walked to my happy place and melted down.

While ordering, someone in the queue asked an innocuous question about the weather, the football, I really can't remember, and I wobbled emotionally. *Please let the ground swallow me up,* I thought. My lungs seemed to spasm and clench, my breathing shortened, and I felt the all-too-familiar sensations of an oncoming panic attack. As it lurched up at me, a sheen of sweat drizzled down my back. My senses became overstimulated. Every nerve buzzed with pins and needles. I was suddenly sensitive to the too-strong smell of coffee, a baby crying nearby, and the bitter acidity on my taste buds. Then my heart rate accelerated. Unable to look the barista in the eye, I staggered to the nearest table and tried to calm down as the self-doubting whispers returned:

Why are you doing this?

Where are you going to go once this is done?

Who are you now?

Then the whispering grew into a shout: *WHAT THE FUCK DO YOU WANT?*

I felt like a human hand grenade, angry and potentially explosive. I couldn't understand what was happening to me. *Why wasn't I over this already?* I thought, as I left in a flap and returned to the hotel. Once inside my room, I locked myself in the bathroom. I wanted to protect my body and soul from the outside world.

'When you get back on The Path, you'll be OK,' I said out loud, hoping it was true.

The following day, I went to the doctor's on the instruction of a concerned mate who had listened to my frazzled story on the phone and kindly paid for more nights at the hotel. Expecting to receive a diagnosis of physical burnout, the physician instead gave me a clean bill of health.

'If anything, you're as fit as a fiddle,' she said. 'Which leads me to believe your issue is mental rather than medical.'

I was then ordered to rest for a few more days. But really, only one course of treatment was going to put things right.

I had to get back on The Path.

* * *

The West Highland Way was exactly the calming experience I'd hoped for. At its starting point in Milngavie, the sights, sounds and smells of Glasgow became an afterthought. Everything was so green and vivid. A track curved its way towards a range of hills and mountains, wisps of thin cloud hanging from their peaks, all shrouded browns, purples and greys. Spring was really kicking in now. A warm sun glowed through the valley; the gorse and grass bent under the weight of a chilly morning dew, and shards of refracted rainbow light beamed through the last gasps of an overnight mist like little flickering lens flares. It was as if I'd emerged from Professor Digory Kirke's wardrobe and stepped into a real-world Narnia. The view was all fantasy cinema – I half expected a white witch to appear in the fog or a weird, winged beast to swoop into view.

And then I saw the stag.

It crested the hill ahead of me, a dark silhouette set against the sky, its unmistakable shadow motionless and jagged. And as I watched it sniff the air and survey the landscape nervously, I was transported back to that terrifying first night in Lulworth Cove when an ominous shape, all angular bone and muscular limbs, had blocked out the stars. Back then, the animal's arrival had pressed on my fears and uncertainties. Now it felt like a reassuring totem – of strength, rejuvenation and enlightenment. *It's a sign that everything's going to be OK,* I thought, feeling a weird jolt of adrenaline as I started jogging towards it, entirely unsure of what might happen once I'd closed the distance or how to behave in the beast's presence. Those antlers looked fearsome.

But I'd moved too fast. Spooked by my approach, the stag sniffed the air again and then stepped backwards, dropping out of sight. Annoyed, I rested at a nearby boulder but when I looked around, I noticed another one was chewing at the grass on the trail ahead. One more had perched on a hill to my left. Then the biggest stag yet wandered casually behind me, almost within touching distance. *They were bloody everywhere!*

I'd seemingly been dropped into an advert for the Scottish Tourist Board and the presence of these amazing animals was incredibly stabilising. I was reminded of those moments as a Royal Marine when I'd stepped onto land for the first time after several weeks on a tipping vessel at sea.

The other thing the West Highland Way wasn't short on was trekkers. They peppered the trail ahead, small moving dots in dayglo Gore-Tex. I later learned that some of them had travelled from as far away as America. One 88-year-old man, a Seattleite, was walking the route with his daughter. It had long been his dream to complete the West Highland Way and with time running out, he'd decided to finally give it a go. A few days later, at the bottom of the Devil's Staircase – a mountain ridge that marked Glen Coe's northern ledge – I met a German couple, Max and Nadine. We walked together for 48 hours, sharing coffee and camping on the side of the track. Several months later, I was told that their first child had been conceived in a tent shortly after I'd left them.

Everyone I spoke to seemed at peace because it was almost impossible to be uptight and angry in such a scenic world. My headspace calmed and tuned into an altogether different frequency, where I discovered the time to think, problem solve and plan. Walking in the still air, I realised, was a purpose all in itself, especially when it connected me to other people. A communal bond was created with the other walkers (especially over a coffee or a hipflask of whisky), and there was a feeling of shared suffering (especially in rough weather) and achievement (especially after a long day). There were no demands, no expectations and no judgements. Really, authenticity and trust were the only currencies, and their exchange united people that ordinarily wouldn't have crossed paths: men, women and kids of all ages, backgrounds and beliefs walked the West Highland Way. It didn't matter if someone was walking a few kilometres or all 154 of them. The important thing was that they were *doing it*.

Set against the mountain tops, I became insignificant, a speck on the landscape. But surrendering to that idea felt empowering, as it had done on the South West Coast Path, and I imagined how these lands had remained unchanged for thousands and thousands of years, and why, in comparison, my life was a fleeting blip and should be savoured. Meanwhile, the messages I'd received over the past two years were making more sense. That engraving in Exeter Cathedral: *Memento mori*, or 'Remember you will die'. Nicola's chat at the kitchen table: 'You need to figure out your *enough*.' And the advice from an old lady, my first encounter on The Path: 'You should feel good about it. *About you*.' By the time I'd neared the West Highland Way's finishing point, I was feeling excited by my situation again, rather than terrified, but it took other people to really confirm that there had been any change at all.

They say that a person's energy often speaks before they do, and it can arrive in many ways – body language, mindset, even ego. Mine was transforming and that truth was now being beamed back at me by everyone else on The Path. Walkers shouted comments when I waved out to them. They wanted to know why I was so happy. They asked how I had so much energy, where my enthusiasm was coming from, and – if I had some to spare – would I mind lending it out? I could have told them the truth: that I was as scared of the future, as anxious about money and as down on the state of the world as everybody else. Instead, I thanked them for their compliments and kept on walking, knowing that in receiving their kind words, rather than brushing them off with suspicion or a self-deprecating joke, I was meeting my true self for the very first time.

Even my way of talking had changed. Before trekking The Path, I was known for clamming up in conversations. Whenever I had something to say, it was delivered at a hundred miles an hour, in the hope that I might reach the end of a thought without embarrassing myself. The new me was very different, however. I brought confidence to introductions, my thinking was clear in discussions, and small talk came easily. I was officially a chatty bugger.

By the time I'd walked under the brooding peak of Ben Nevis and yomped the final yards to Fort William, I was relieved. It didn't bother me anymore that the people I'd grown up with or served alongside were now married with kids, mortgages and careers. The FOMO had gone. I was chuffed for them and chuffed for me, doing my thing and happy to be walking around Britain. I felt proud.

That sense of security might have had something to do with my location. Having officially passed the halfway mark in my journey, the fastest route home was now ahead of me, rather than in my rear-view mirror. To get back to Bournemouth, I had to first boot it around the remainder of Scotland, before trekking the beaches and coastal trails of Northumberland and Lincolnshire, Anglia, Essex and Kent. Fading away in the distance were the Lakes, Chester, Wales and the South West

Coast Path. The hardest yards had been done. Just knowing that had a powerful effect.

But I also felt protected because I was being magnetised to a powerful and loving memory. Every time I opened my wallet, I noticed the dog-eared photo of my grandparents on their boat trip to Skye. Wherever I walked, Nan's locket bounced across my chest. Every glimpse and sensation seemed to poke at me like an alert on my phone.

The Isle of Skye.

All roads led to it.

CHAPTER TWELVE

A RESTING PLACE

I wanted closure on my grandparents' passing. The idea had been nagging at me since that first trip to Nicola and David's, when I'd talked about their familial love, our lives together and the concept of maybe finding my *enough*. The more I thought about it, the more attuned I became to the idea of burying Nan's locket on Skye. It was the perfect forward step and once I got there, my plan was to scour the island for somewhere special – a spot important to her or us. The idea intensified whenever I thought about my final heartbreaking phone call to Nan several years ago. Me working a million miles away as a teacher in Thailand; her on her hospital bed, out of reach. My cousin had held his phone close to Nan's ear as I'd tried to comfort her on the other end of the line, but my words were inaudible. The end was too close for her and I was too choked up.

'I love you,' I said, not really believing this could be our last conversation.

I was in denial. And having been unable to hold Nan's hand or hug her one last time, I became crushed under a wave of guilt and grief.

Several years on, that pain was an exposed nerve. It ached whenever I thought about her, but there was always hope. The Path had presented me with one or two moments of closure already: one for Dad, one for my place in the world. *So, would Skye be another?* All I wanted was for the healing process to accelerate and the hurt to dissipate, though I had no idea where to bury Nan's locket or whether to add a ceremonial flourish to the occasion, like a reading or moonlit vigil. (Or something.) Whenever the subject came up in conversations with Nicola, David or anyone else, the consensus was that I should take my time and not worry about the pre-planning. Apparently, good old-fashioned gut instinct was my most reliable guide.

'You'll know the place when you see it,' said one café Yoda, over drinks. 'You'll feel it.'

'I bloody well hope so,' I sighed, not feeling convinced.

I pulled on the locket every day. It was now part of me and I wondered whether its absence might disconnect me from Nan in some way or muddle my emotional compass. I'd likely feel naked without it for a while; at that point in my life, the metal was almost a physical extension of my body. Then I remembered that possessions and their perceived value – financial, emotional or otherwise – had never been my thing. As far as I was concerned, people and places mattered the most in life, not jewellery or trinkets. And while Nan's locket had occasionally brought reassurance, especially during moments of stress, I knew that placing it somewhere symbolic was probably for the best. It would permanently bond her to a location she'd loved and numb my hurt and guilt at her passing. From now on, I wanted to remember Nan and Grandad for the good times.

She'd have loved you doing this walk, I thought, as I rested in Fort William, where it was so hard to relax. After the West Highland Way, Skye was the next destination on my route, and Nan and her locket poked at me for days, until I eventually trekked to the harbour village of Mallaig – a small outpost cut into a series of bright green hills that swept down to the shoreline. The plan was to catch the ferry to Armadale in the south of the island and walk north. But the omens were bad. When I arrived in Mallaig, the rain was coming in at right angles. The sea outside my hotel window churned and chopped, and as I fell asleep, it was hard to shake the idea that a rough crossing was in store. That's if the ferries were running at all. But the morning brought in a whole other mood: when I anxiously opened the curtains, the sky was bright blue and the sea pondwater still. This was the idyllic island life from my rose-tinted memories.

I tightened up my Bergen and plodded towards the ferry. Later, as it turned and swayed towards Armadale, I stared at the town in the distance, trying to connect with my past. I imagined the boy who'd once hung out there with his nan and grandad. *I mean, how long ago was it?* My best guess placed the year as 1996. I'd been 13 years old back then and obsessed with football, especially Manchester United, once the biggest team in the world. My hormones had been raging too and I'd become increasingly aware of the girls in my classroom. Never mind kissing one, just knowing they existed was both intoxicating and life-changing, and I'd dreamed of a moment when I might get to hang out with somebody from the opposite sex. *Maybe I'd find her on Skye?*

Laughing, I took another look at the photo in my wallet. *What was I thinking?* No chance was that happening on a trip to Scotland with those two. Then I stared at the Armadale of 25-plus years later, as a small pod of dolphins breached in the harbour. A knot of emotion grew in my throat.

'Bloody hell,' I said. 'Skye's giving me a proper welcome here . . .'

I felt transported, instantly nostalgic for the good times and the nearly forgotten. My overwhelming feeling was that our 1996 holiday had been a restorative experience. I don't remember there being any complaints from me when Nan had first announced the trip. It freed me from my turbulent domestic life and school playground hell, so I was more like a prisoner on day release than a sulky teen. I also knew that Nan and Grandad were ushering me into a magical world of craggy mountains, rocky beaches and fairy pools – Skye's mystical-looking waterfalls and natural swimming holes that gurgled and shimmered like living picture postcards. Nan believed the island, and its icy waters, would have the same healing effect on my frazzled brain as it'd had on theirs in the past. They'd loved Skye so much.

I did too, Nan.

I pulled at the locket on my neck again and smiled. 'Bet you didn't think I'd come back,' I said quietly.

Then I stepped into Armadale, hoping to find the perfect moment.

* * *

Physically, I was on point. I'd been walking for the best part of a year, minus the interruptions; my calf muscles were pumped and my thighs flexed and pushed like pistons. Mentally, I'd developed a bombproof level of self-belief, especially when it came to my resilience. When I unfolded an old paper map of Skye on the harbour wall and looked at its mass, steep inclines and jagged terrain, I barely flinched. There was a little fear, yeah. But when the going got tough, I knew my elite mindset would do the heavy lifting. Feeling determined, I began my yomp across the island. The intention for the next few days was to move from south to north as I tried to locate a suitable burial spot.

Summer had arrived; the weather was unseasonably warm. And as I left the concrete and car parks of Armadale's ferry port and stepped into the gorse and long grass outside, the heat enveloped me. The trail ahead looked scorched; a light wind occasionally whispered across the green-brown landscape. Then everything exploded with insects. *Midges*. Angry, almost invisible bugs that swarmed over my flesh, feasting on any exposed gaps in my fabric armour. Even though I'd bought a long-sleeve top and a special hat (the shop assistant had even praised its anti-midge protective net as I'd handed over my card), the bastards were small and determined. There were millions of them and a dark cloud formed around me. They attacked the small spaces of skin on the back of my neck, wrists and ankles. And with every bite, I itched and tickled for hours afterwards.

I walked for a full day in the wide-brimmed, anti-midge hat and the heat became almost unbearable. I was claustrophobic under the dark netting. My breath was held in the lining, which raised the temperature and smothered my face. I was sweating hard and it pooled in my pits and bits. In a journey comprising thousands of miles and a long list of abandoned home comforts, this was possibly the most disgusting I had felt.

I stink, I thought. *I need to wash.*

I looked at my watch. It was 7pm and still bright. The long summer evenings meant I could probably walk until ten or 11 o'clock, but it was dinner time and I'd planned on camping for the first night. Having pitched my tent, I spotted a small pool of still water. Then, with nobody in view, I stripped down to my pants and rummaged about in my Bergen for some soap and a towel. Talk about a schoolboy error. More midges swarmed around me. They must have had a similar feeding pattern to humans. Breakfast was served at 7am, dinner at 7pm and snacking was encouraged everywhere in between. I'd exposed my body and scent at the worst possible time, and another large black mass instantly swallowed me whole. Lashing out was impossible, like punching at smoke, and the cloud writhed and distorted about my flailing limbs. When I eventually sunk into the water, my arms, legs and back bumped with tiny, irritating bites. Then the insect army feasted on my head and scalp like it was an all-you-can-eat buffet. I scratched and seethed in my tent for hours afterwards, cursing my stupidity.

And still there was nowhere suitable to leave Nan's locket.

The following day, I walked from sun up, making sure to protect every square centimetre of my body from the insects, scanning the horizon for a suitable burial place, only to come up short. My gut instinct was failing me. Then, after a third full day on the trail, having reached Uig in the northwest of

Skye, I settled in a pub garden for a dinner of beer and crisps. The sunlight danced across the tide in the distance and I mulled over the now burning question of a suitable resting place for Nan.

Suddenly, a voice called out from behind me: 'Here, I drove past you. Hours ago.'

When I looked up, a tall man with a shock of wild, white hair was setting his pint glass down on the next table. Several of his friends were deep in conversation nearby. He nodded at me knowingly. 'Yeah, miles back,' he confirmed. 'Walking. Through the midges. What the bloody hell are you doing?'

I laughed. Then I told him about The Path, where I'd been so far and my plan to bury Nan's locket somewhere on Skye. The bloke (whose name I now can't remember) stared incredulously.

'That's some trip, pal,' he said. 'You're having a drink and I'm buying.'

He plonked a frothy beer in front of me. 'Tell me more . . .'

My new friend was a rich source of local intel, as were his mates. I was eventually pointed in the direction of a nearby campsite and as I desperately pulled my tent together, a light shower soaking my clothes and kit, the midges came alive again. My mind flitted between frustration and inspiration. I was disappointed, having failed to find a suitable place for Nan's locket, but my wheels were spinning at a suitable alternative: the Isle of Harris, one half of the Outer Hebridean island Lewis and Harris. The outpost had been suggested by the white-haired man and his friends, plus several others online. Everybody who'd mentioned it also recommended the Calanais Standing Stones, a cruciform of eerie, rocky monoliths that seemed to sprout from the earth and were thought to have been planted there 5,000 years ago, a time before Stonehenge.

I checked the map. Harris was only a ferry ride away. And when I then investigated the Calanais Standing Stones, my heart thumped. The rocks were as ethereal as everyone had described, and several myths had been connected to them. In winter, a low moon danced around the peaks and tops, leading some people to believe they worked as a primitive observatory. From a distance, the rocks either curled up to the sky like gnarled fingers or resembled spectral beings set against the bleak greens, greys and purples of the nearby mountains. The grounds apparently had a supernatural atmosphere, as if some powerful force was operating nearby. As I scrolled through the pictures, my stomach tightened with butterflies. I felt it.

This was the perfect spot for Nan's locket.

Calanais was the breakthrough I'd been hoping for and it presented a massive uptick in emotions. My day had been an unsettling, emotional rollercoaster, punctuated with wrong turns, false dawns and rude interruptions. Whenever I'd stepped into an area of reception, my phone had pinged noisily with texts and alerts. Nearly all of them mentioned the political turmoil unfolding in Afghanistan, my workplace for two years. The country was undergoing a distressing geopolitical changeover and in April, Joe Biden, the then US President, had announced that America's troops would be leaving the country before 11 September 2021, the twentieth anniversary of the horrific terrorist attacks on the World Trade Center in New York. The Taliban, for so long a military adversary, were set to fill the leadership vacuum, and their regime was reportedly intent on returning Afghanistan's people to a dictatorial, almost medieval, rule.

I checked the calendar. September was looming and the unfolding events made me feel sick. So many British lives had been lost during the Allied occupation of Afghanistan but it was my opinion that the country had been better off as a result of our presence. During that time, the Taliban had been displaced and the atmosphere of oppression, for so long their number-one method of leadership, had been reduced. Women were allowed to walk the streets without burkhas. Kids learned about the world beyond their borders. New forms of technology and healthcare had been introduced to the population. But the Taliban's reemergence would usher in a terrifying return to the old ways. The nation was scared.

I knew that because I still had friends there, local mates from my time spent working on the ground as a contractor from 2012 to 2014. The imminent regime changes meant revenge attacks on anyone who had previously opposed the Taliban – and there were plenty of targets. I thought of the driver I'd worked with, Habib. He was likely to be on their hitlist because it had been our job to escort government officials around Kabul as they flitted from meeting to meeting. Some of them had been key members of Hillary Clinton's team and the work was undoubtedly high-risk. We were watched everywhere we went. The Taliban, while a defeated presence at that point, still lurked in the shadows. Not that it bothered me; I was familiar with the people, culture and rhythms of Kabul, the capital city, and I loved exploring its markets and the hidden coffee shops and cafés, especially when mixing with locals I knew to be trustworthy.

Sometimes, though, my bravado got the better of me. One day, I asked Habib to take me to a market in a nearby village. I'd heard it was a wild scene.

Habib shook his head. 'No, Mr Paul, we'll get in trouble.'

'It's OK, bro,' I said, laughing. 'We'll be totally fine. Who's going to mind?'

Habib wasn't having it. 'But it's dangerous—'

'Come on, I'm calling it. We're going!'

Reluctantly, Habib started the car. When we arrived, the market lived up to its edgy reputation. The place buzzed with an outlandish, otherworldly energy. Animal carcasses smoked over pits of blazing charcoal. Vendors traded rugs, herbs and fabrics. The hairs on my neck prickled – a sure sign I was being watched by someone in the darkness. Every alcove brimmed with a dark energy and I felt instantly out of place, like a *Star Wars* character entering a lawless galactic spaceport – a dusty, beaten-up outpost packed with bounty hunters, traders and pirates. I noticed a bundle of grenades in a basket stashed under a trader's table and did a double take. Someone was holding an AK-47 and my Spidey senses tickled. Once I'd spotted one knife, everyone seemed to be carrying them. Habib was probably right: I was taking a risk and the chances of me getting shot, stabbed or blown up were higher there than anywhere else. But I didn't care. Everything was going to be OK.

I felt a tug on my arm. It was Habib. 'Please, Mr Paul, I think this place is dangerous.'

It's hard to explain but I felt utterly fearless at that point in my life. It wasn't as if I had a death wish, I certainly didn't want to get hurt, but I can't recall any anxiety or adrenaline.

Instead, there was an undeniable sense of freedom to everything I did, like I was expanding the boundaries of my life in places I'd likely never visit again. This was a massive mindset shift from 2012, during my first few weeks in Afghanistan. Back then, I'd been hyper-vigilant, which was undoubtedly a result of my military training. Whenever I stepped outside our compound, I would nervously scan the walls and rooftops of every building, my weapon raised. Then one day, a teammate pulled me aside. He'd been working in Kabul for a long time.

'Chill out, mate,' he said. 'Lower your weapon. It's not *Call of Duty*. Everything's cool.'

My behaviour back then had been over the top. But two years later, I'd become dangerously complacent. My afternoon of naïve indifference in the market soon came to an end when we drove away to a place nicknamed TV Hill because of its popularity as a background with reporters as they broadcasted their daily reports. Then the phone buzzed. It was my boss, Warren.

'Where have you been?'

I told him of my trip to the market, the basket of grenades and a nearby AK-47. Then he freaked out.

'Stay the fuck away from there!' he shouted.

'What? Why?'

'Because it's controlled by the Taliban, you idiot!'

His reaction was jolting, like a bucket of ice-cold water over the head, and I instantly sharpened up. *What was I thinking?*

I turned to Habib. 'You were right,' I said, cursing my nonchalance. 'We shouldn't have gone.'

From what I can remember, moments like those, plus the

beheading of our company finance clerk, were outliers. For the most part, post-war Afghanistan was a beautiful place. Aside from the Taliban, the people were warm and friendly, and hyper-aware of their reputation beyond the borders. They felt the same way about their terrorist oppressors as we did and a lot of them yearned for a return to the 1960s, when their homeland had been a vibrant destination on the hippy trail, and Kabul was an exotically cosmopolitan city that weirdly echoed some of the West's opulence and creativity. The characters I worked with, like Habib, were underdogs, diamonds in the rough. The Afghanistan I experienced was a lesson in propaganda: *Don't believe what you read in the papers*. While the Afghan people I met were a lesson in humanity – kind, caring and enchanting. Knowing they were being abandoned to a cruel and brutal ruler broke my heart.

I texted Habib, hoping he was OK. Then I settled down in my tent for the night, thankful that the only thing I had to fear in Scotland were the midges. An early wake-up call for the morning ferry awaited.

Harris on Harris. Nan would have loved it.

CHAPTER THIRTEEN

RIPPLES INTO WAVES

When I'd first set out on The Path, traversing the Scottish islands hadn't been a part of my plans. But suddenly, here they were, in sharp focus, and I seemed to be living on the edge of the world. On Lewis and Harris, as with Skye, the sea was Thailand blue, the vegetation rainforest green. The roads were empty – there were no cars or bikes, no houses or crofts. Nothing stirred on the horizon and upon arriving, I felt instantly and beautifully alone. Under a jagged, rocky skyline and blazing sun, I imagined being stranded on another planet, a character in a sci-fi movie. It was at once eerie and oddly romantic.

I thought back to the wild adventures of Dorset alumnus Lawrence of Arabia, as I had done during my tipping point moment at those Roman ruins near Basingstoke. When he'd explored far-flung locations, his stories would go untold for months, even years, and his letters, when they appeared in one of the national newspapers, felt like important events. It was the early twentieth-century equivalent of a YouTube vlog: a pioneering explorer sharing his stories through missives to the likes of Noël Coward, Winston Churchill or George Bernard Shaw. The lightning speed of information 100 years later would have probably blown his mind. I scrolled through my phone, uploaded another photo and marked my position on Instagram's GPS.

Almost the minute I'd confirmed my visit to Lewis and Harris, an accommodation offer had arrived from the owners of Harris's Temple Café. A similar thing had happened on Skye, when Andrew and Rich from The Coffee Bothy in Broadford had kindly offered their spare room as a sleeping spot. After checking the café's social media, I'd drooled. The Coffee Bothy menu was impressive: one photo proudly showed off a display case stacked with chocolate brownies and carrot cakes, some of which looked worthy of a Hollywood Handshake on *The Great British Bake Off*. In another, a plate of doorstep toast had been topped with two perfectly poached eggs. Their bright orange yolks oozed across the dark crust and pooled against a small reservoir of melting butter. At that point, my stomach grumbled noisily.

These invitations always brought a massive surge of relief. I felt less exposed, safer; plus a house meant respite from the midges. But also, every guaranteed night of civilisation led me towards a new connection, a new friend and a fresh ally, and I'd learned that every altruistic soul had a story to tell. The Coffee Bothy owners were perfect examples. Rich had been working as cabin crew for a major airline when Covid hit and he was cut loose in a wave of redundancies. Meanwhile, Andrew – a science teacher living in Edinburgh – was breaking up with his wife after coming out as gay. He'd then met Rich and found happiness, the perfect ending to a lifetime of hiding. The pair of them later opened The Coffee Bothy.

Meanwhile, Julian and Amanda from the Temple Café had moved from Sussex to Harris with the dream of opening a coffee shop. Judging by their photos, they'd landed in the perfect location. Their immediate view was beautiful, all loch and mountain peaks. The building was bizarre, a domed shack built from stacked stone, and its exterior resembled the house owned by Bilbo Baggins in *The Hobbit*. Its insides were just as striking. Curved wooden beams framed the ceiling like the guts of an upturned rowing boat. A knotted tree trunk, a striking structural support, curled towards the roof. At the heart of the building was a wooden bar, a centrepiece engraved with etchings of flowers and plants. Small mountains of carrot cakes, cruffins and millionaire shortbread were piled up on top.

I was always amazed at how unknown hosts would go the extra yard. Amanda and Julian, then strangers, had wanted to know whether I had a favourite meal. (And could they cook it?) Did I want a packed lunch for the following day? And was there anything else they could do for me, like laundry? As always, I had very little in the way of personal requests, apart from one. *Nobody washes my underwear but me*. I was mortified at the thought of stranger handling my sweaty pants, especially when they were putting me up for a night or two.

As I walked the opening kilometres across Harris, Julian and Amanda sent me directions to the Temple Café. But their simple instructions had gone over my head for some reason and along the way, I took a wrong turn. Realising my error,

I checked the map and fumed at my clumsiness. I was further away from the coffee shop than when I started by 10 kilometres or so.

It was a boiling hot day. The late summer sun was intense and my mood was being soured by the day's football results. Manchester United had been spanked by Brentford. As I tried to calm myself in the quiet, Amanda, wondering why I'd taken so long to complete a relatively short journey – me being a serious walker and all – texted with the offer of a lift. I looked around at the remote landscape. The view was stunning, all sea, mountains and long grasses. The silence utterly alien. I was having too much of a moment. Besides, I'd got myself into this sticky predicament; it was down to me to escape it. The only way to do that was to keep on walking. I turned down Amanda's kind offer and pressed ahead.

Sometimes, the implications of a bad decision reveal them-selves almost instantly. Not 20 minutes after Amanda's text, the sun reached its highest point and I wilted in the heat. My Bergen felt bulkier than before; my trail shoes became concrete heavy. Amanda, presumably watching the intensifying conditions from the Temple Café, returned with an improved offer:

Paul, how about I come to you, pick up your big rucksack? Then you can walk for the rest of the day with a smaller bag.

This time, I was much more receptive. 'That sounds great,' I replied. 'Where shall I meet you?'

Amanda suggested a suitable point on the map, though it came with an ominous warning. Apparently, I wasn't to take the next right turn. Doing so would lead me up a vertiginous hill and I'd likely collapse with exhaustion. 'It'll kill you,' wrote Amanda, making her point more clearly. I laughed wryly. The Royal Marines loved a challenge and she had presented me with a do-or-die moment.

'We had a saying in the military,' I wrote. 'You can rest once you've got to the top of a hill. I'll meet you there.'

According to Amanda, I was mad. And she was right. The climb was horrific, the trail leading up and away, seemingly forever, but I pressed on regardless. My throat became sore with dehydration. My brain was unable to make basic decisions through exhaustion, such as where to pause and when to take a sip of water. It must have taken me 20 minutes to get to the top and as I pushed forward, head down, my hands gripped the straps of my Bergen tightly for support. I counted every step silently, looking up every time I reached 50 as a way of gauging my progress. Yes, I could have dropped my bag and waited for Amanda on the roadside, but I felt accountable. Cutting corners or taking the easy way out wasn't my style. A masochistic streak ran through me. I wanted to push myself to breaking point, if only to understand where my breaking point had been set. Then I wanted to brush past it.

There was a boulder in the distance and I marked it a brief resting spot. Striding forward aggressively, like a donkey being led by a dangling carrot, I heard the faint growling of a motorbike in the distance. This was the first vehicle I'd encountered in hours and when it eventually roared past me, the rider turned back. He was staring in disbelief and I couldn't blame him. With my huge bag and sweat-soaked kit, I made for a freakish sight. Having reached the boulder, the biker turned around, killed the engine and shouted, but I couldn't hear a word he was saying from under his visor.

I stepped towards him cautiously. When the rider took off his helmet, there was a powerful sense of recognition.

I knew him.

'I fucking know you,' shouted the rider.

Stunned, I nodded. It was Mark, my former troop sergeant from my time at Her Majesty's Naval Base Clyde, or Faslane as it was known during my time. The Royal Navy's nest of hunter-killer submarines had been stationed there.

Mark shook his head. 'Bloody hell! Faslane. 2003?'

I laughed. 'Yeah, I was there between 2003 and 2005. You were my troop sergeant.'

Mark dismounted, pulled off his riding gloves, and shook my hand. 'So, what the bloody hell are you doing, yomping about Harris and Lewis, Royal?'

Once I'd finished my now well-edited spiel, I mentioned that Amanda, the owner of the Temple Café, was coming by shortly to pick me up. Mark shook his head.

'Of course! She mentioned you the other day. Said something about a Marine walking around Britain. Coming here. She wanted to know whether I knew you.'

I heard the beep of a car horn. With impeccable timing, Amanda had pulled up alongside us.

'See? I told you!' she laughed, winding down the window and gesturing for me to put my bag in the boot. Then she shoved a bottle of ice-cold water into my hand.

'End of the day, Royal?' said Mark, helping me to heave the load from my back.

'No way! I'm walking all the way to their coffee shop.'

He nodded at Amanda. 'You going to let him? That's fucking miles!'

She shrugged. I'd already worn her down with my stubborn attitude. 'I tried. But he's not changing his mind.'

Mark lifted the seat of his bike. A bag of chocolate bars had been stuffed into the storage space. 'Well, in that case, take these,' he said, shoving them at me. 'My missus is a nutritionist. She's sworn me off the stuff but I've kept a little stash. You're going to need them more than me.'

After they both disappeared over the other side of the hill, their horns beeping, the self-flagellation continued. I walked for hours, wondering if I'd bitten off more than I could chew. When I later rounded a golf course and checked my position on the map, I'd yomped a total of 30 kilometres during the day. Everything ached. My socks and shorts were soaked through with sweat and I stank like a goat farmer. When Amanda passed by with another bottle of water, I refused her second offer of a lift. I was fixed on the finish line and with only 2 kilometres to go, I had it in me to complete the journey before sunset. Stubbornly, I pressed ahead.

Minutes later, another car slowed ahead of me. This time it was Mark. He was leaning out of the window.

'Royal! *Enough,*' he shouted. 'Get in the fucking wagon now! You can pick up from here tomorrow.'

I opened the door and sat, exhausted, in the passenger seat. Turning down help from a civilian was one thing. No way was I refusing an order.

* * *

For a couple of days, still feeling exhausted, I whiled away the hours, drinking coffee and sharing stories with Mark, Julian and Amanda. Mark was now a mountain climbing instructor and travelled across Europe with his clients. Julian, an academic, had previously taught refugees living in the UK, a service he'd long offered for free. Some of his students had fled from the Taliban. One morning, he wanted to know what I thought about the military withdrawal from Afghanistan.

'Like, what's the point?' I said, nihilistically. The geopolitical climate had put me in a dark mood. 'What's the point of anything?'

Mark looked concerned. 'What do you mean by that?'

'Well, we've both been there,' I said, trying not to become too emotional. 'I lost friends. You probably did too. Now we've given the Taliban free rein to drag the country back to the Middle Ages. It's horrible. We do all these things and then someone, somewhere, just decides that they're gonna rip up the script. So, what's the point?'

Julian shook his head. 'That's not true,' he said eventually.

'What do you mean?'

'Well, it could be true,' he continued. 'But it doesn't have to be. How you do things and what you say can make a massive change. It affects things in a good way.'

'Like, how?'

'By not listening to the negativity,' said Julian, now refilling the coffees. 'Not buying into it. You are your own world. You are in charge. But you can only affect what you can affect. You can't change the situation in Afghanistan – not on your own. But if you say good things, do good things and believe in good things, then slowly, you'll affect the people around you. Slowly, those people will change too. The ripples you make will eventually turn into waves.'

I shrugged. *Maybe.*

'No, definitely,' said Julian forcefully. 'We can all make magic. All of us.'

I sipped my coffee, Julian's words not quite sinking in. It was a nice sentiment for sure but hardly a tangible strategy for the Real World. As we debated, customers came and went in a blur. Everyone in the Temple Café seemed to know one another. With each familiar face, Mark pointed to me: *You want to hear about this guy.* I must have retold my story a dozen times over. Eventually, a woman waved out. She had been sitting in the corner and I'd noticed her scribbling on a piece of paper. Now she was handing it over.

'You're probably going to come through Edinburgh,' she said, in a half question, half statement. 'When you do, stay with us. We'd love to have you.'

When I later opened the note, Mark whistled. 'You're basically crashing in the Chelsea of Edinburgh.'

Bloody hell.

'Happen to you a lot, does it?' he said, nodding at the woman now leaving the café. 'Random people offering up their houses?'

Well, yeah. 'All the time.'

Julian leaned over. He was smiling.

'There you go,' he said, patting me gently on the back. 'Ripples into waves.'

* * *

I buried Nan's locket a few days later, having visited the Calanais Standing Stones in Callanish, the northern part of Lewis and Harris. It was a beautiful morning. A heavy mist steamed away under the sun, and as I approached the cruciform of crooked stone blocks, each one a jagged, twisted limb that pointed skywards, I was transported into an almost fantasy world of historical warriors and ancient cultures. The type of stuff I'd only really seen in old films.

I'd always been fascinated by the Romans. The Vikings too. Part of that had a lot to do with my military background. These were warrior cultures that believed in honour, tradition and stoicism. The Vikings cherished the idea of living a good life and dying a noble, courageous death. It was seen as the only way to reach Valhalla, their version of heaven. Whenever I walked through a historical site, whether that be Roman, Viking or neolithic, like the Calanais Standing Stones, I experienced a weird rush of energy, as if I'd connected with something supernatural or religious. Maybe even the universe. When I passed a monument or rocky circle that was known to have been constructed by an ancient civilisation, my problems – a life without direction, a series of familial disappointments, the breakdown of a relationship that I'd thought was my forever – felt insignificant. I was a blip in time. Whether I was in a scientific or spiritual mood, it was impossible not to feel humbled by the grand scale of the cosmos. If I could, I'd lay a hand on the stonework or stand as close as the boundary would allow. 'I need the energy of a warrior,' I'd say. 'Give it to me. I want to feel it.' Then I'd give thanks for the now.

The emotional boost that followed was like a power-up in a

video game – a super leaf or fire flower from *Super Mario Kart*. It kept me going for hours afterwards.

I received a similar burst of energy as I approached the circle of rocks at Calanais. Over the past few days, I'd heard all sorts of stories about its meaning and design. When viewed from above, the stones made the shape of a cross; from another perspective, their jagged tops were said to resemble a woman lying on her back. Sometimes, as the moon moved across the sky, its curvature was supposed to create an optical illusion along the peaks: the woman became pregnant; the full moon was her belly. The place was steeped in mythology and pagan rituals. It was mystical. Which made it the perfect place to bury Nan's locket.

I heard the voices of everyone who'd advised me to follow my gut instinct.

Then I got digging.

I grabbed a small, fist-sized stone from the nearby trail and checked the horizon for any approaching walkers. Satisfied I wouldn't be disturbed for a while, I got down on my hands and knees and gouged a deep hole in the ground. Then I placed the locket at the bottom.

'This is the place, Nan,' I said quietly.

I piled the dirt on top gently. 'This is my way of letting go.'

When the hole was filled, I carefully smoothed over the surface, patting down any raised edges. No one passing by would have been able to tell that the earth had been disturbed.

'I've been hanging onto this, *to you*, for years,' I continued. 'You've had such a powerful hold on me. But life needs to go on. You said that to me once . . .'

I remembered the moment clearly and again pictured the two

of us in Nan's kitchen as she urged me to go to Thailand. 'This is life,' she said. 'I don't want you to stop living on my account. You need to keep moving forward.'

I smiled at the memory. 'So, I'm still moving forward, Nan,' I said, getting to my feet. 'I love you. I always will. I've just got some things to figure out now – and I've got to do it alone.'

Then I walked away, at peace, leaving behind a special person in a special place.

CHAPTER FOURTEEN

A NORTHERN SOUL

Having left Lewis and Harris and taken the ferry to Ullapool, on the mainland, I connected with the wild and remote North Coast 500. When planning my journey in 2020, this was the region I'd most feared: the trails in this part of the country seemed to have been cut off from the rest of civilisation, almost forgotten, and as soon as I arrived, I felt vulnerable and dangerously isolated. Churning tides crashed against the shoreline, the nearby hills were smothered in dark, pregnant cloud banks, and several eagles circled overhead, scanning the landscape for their next dinner. Set against this dramatic backdrop, I was a moving target for nature at its most vicious.[2]

But even in these isolated nooks on the British map, I had

---

2 Around this time, I left The Path for a European holiday, which was kindly paid for by the former Navy SEAL, author and podcast host, Marcus Luttrell. I was invited onto his show and then, in an act of amazing generosity, he asked me to accompany him and his family for their holiday to Rome. When I told him about my financial position, and that I couldn't possibly afford it, Marcus had told me not to stress. It was all accounted for. 'When you make it in life, remember this,' he said. 'Then pay it forward to someone else.' The generosity blew my mind.

a place to stay, in this case Stoer, where an Airbnb host had offered to let me use the spare room in his house. In our chats, he introduced himself as Paul and seemed pleased for the company. Apart from his cat, and the guests that visited the holiday crofts on the property, Paul lived alone. Now in his fifties, he'd spent his past life working for the TV channel *Discovery*, but when his relationship fell apart and lockdown kicked in, Paul had decided to make a massive life change. He drove to Scotland, his possessions crammed into the back of a car, and transformed the two crofts into profitable businesses, all while making a new home for himself. The risk paid off. Post-pandemic, the UK holiday industry was suddenly booming. Paul, who was making hay while the sun shone, looked to be living his best life.

His home was stunning. A homely cottage with an open fireplace and a view from the windows that seemed to go on forever. 'The crofts are booked out most weeks,' he said. 'But you can stay in here for a couple of days.'

He put the kettle on. 'So, what are your plans?' he said.

'Well, I'm walking a large chunk of the NC500. The coastal bits . . .'

Paul looked at me quizzically. 'You know how remote it is around here? The nearest café is an hour away . . . *In the car.*'

I laughed. 'Yeah, but I've got no choice, really.'

'Well, look. I think your story's amazing,' said Paul, pouring out two mugs of coffee. 'I wish I had the courage to do what you're doing. And to be honest, I've been feeling a bit isolated. I saw on one of your posts that you'd sometimes been using a support wagon . . .'

I thought back to the road trips with Gareth in Dale. I wondered how his mum, Ann, was doing. 'Yeah. That was a massive help.'

'Well, if that's something you're still doing, I'd be up for helping.'

What was originally intended to be a weekend stay was immediately upgraded into a five-week residency as Paul became a champion for my cause. The cottage was transformed into a basecamp fit for the NC500, and every morning, at around 5am, he drove me to the previous day's finishing point. Sometimes, the journey took as long as two and a half hours. Once dispatched, I yomped around the coastline in the cold, autumnal weather, the ferocious, driving winds of *The Minch* – the stretch of water that divides the mainland from the Outer Hebrides – sandblasting my face. On some days, the squalls were with me. They acted like rocket fuel as I burned through 50-kilometre days. On others, I was pushed down by the elements and it took every ounce of willpower to battle through the gale.

Emotionally, the work was tough. Other than my temporary housemate, I barely spoke to another human. The silence was smothering and days passed without me meeting another trekker or dog walker. While I walked, Paul returned to his crofts and made the beds, checked on the guests and cleaned the rooms whenever a changeover was scheduled. Then he collected me at the roadside in the evening, in places as far away as Durness or Bettyhill, my thumb raised like a hitchhiker. Some round trips kept him on the tarmac for upwards of ten hours, and I was so grateful for his support.

Through it all, Paul was the dream companion – kind, smart,

funny – and I looked forward to our commutes, when we shared stories and made jokes. He had previously worked in Rome for five years and spoke fluent Italian. The guy was smart, worldly and well read, and the shelves in his house were stacked with great books. I noticed titles by Paulo Coelho, the photographer Rankin and Douglas Stuart. I also came to understand the rhythms of his personality. Paul could be quiet and, on some occasions, he emotionally retreated to a place that seemed beyond reach. A visible shutdown appeared to take place, his operating system set to standby. Sometimes, Paul's energy levels dropped so dramatically it was as if the weight of the world had been hoisted upon his shoulders. But this was understandable. The pace of life in Stoer and Scotland was very different to the one Paul had experienced in London, where he'd worked for a buzzy TV company. On more than one occasion, he admitted to being lonely.

Then, during one car ride, Paul told me that he was gay.

'Cool, bro,' I said, smiling, not feeling in the slightest bit bothered. 'Thank you for sharing that.'

'You're not weirded out?' said Paul. He seemed nervous.

'No, not at all,' I said. 'Maybe several years ago it would have been a different story, because, you know . . .'

Paul looked at me curiously. 'What do you mean by that?'

'Well, don't get me wrong,' I said, 'it wouldn't have really bothered me or anything. But you've got to remember, I was a Marine. I didn't meet many gay people in the military. I lived in an environment where anyone who might have been different, in terms of their sexuality or otherwise, pretty much kept it to themselves, sadly. For a quiet life.'

He nodded. Then I put my hand on his shoulder. 'Besides, there were some pretty big clues,' I said.

Paul was caught off guard. He'd believed his truth had been well hidden. 'Bollocks!' he said, eventually. 'What clues?'

'Well, I've got a pretty good gaydar. Some of the books were a giveaway. You hung out with a lot of stylish men in Rome . . . *The cat.*'

He laughed. 'Now you're taking the piss.'

I just wanted to hug him. The feelgood factor and dopamine that accompanied the meeting of every stranger, and their transformation into a new friend, was a restorative power I'd never comprehended before, especially if they were different to me. In my previous lives, I'd been cocooned in a series of echo chambers. During my military career, I worked alongside macho individuals that were trained up to be unfeeling weapons of war. I became one of them and, at the time, couldn't have imagined myself hanging out with people from the different communities, backgrounds or even free-thinking creatives living off the grid. During my post-reality TV flush of fame, I moved in a bubble of minor celebrities and assumed the free ride would never end. As a schoolteacher living in Thailand, I became the classic ex-pat worker: an individual who enjoyed my distinct differences to the culture around me while seeking the comfort of familiarity in a network of likeminded Brits, Aussies and South Africans. Life was good, but breaking boundaries was hard.

The Path had forced me to reconsider my outlook. I'd met people from different cultures, backgrounds and upbringings to mine. I experienced the values of a proper family life and shared in the love of a supportive home where every member was championed – even the rando bloke in a smelly t-shirt and walking shorts, a huge rucksack slung over his back. I encountered people with different views on religion, philosophy and sexuality to me, and grew as an individual after every connection because there was a very simple lesson to be found within each conversation: despite the culture wars raging around the country, there was more that connected us as a society than divided us, no matter the headlines in the tabloid press or the crap being posted on social media. It's said that travel is the best teacher, though the assumption is that the explorer in question requires a passport if they're to educate themselves in the broad tapestry of humanity. My walk around the country had showed me that these lessons could be found everywhere. We need only be open to connection to absorb them.

Over the next few weeks, the friendship between Paul and I strengthened. He encouraged me to push myself whenever the worsening weather conditions threatened to derail my progress and I became someone for him to confide in. Both of us shared our hopes and fears for the future, without judgement, and in doing so, we offloaded a little more of the emotional baggage weighing us down. Paul also took pride in showing me the Scotland I hadn't expected to see. One night, as I readied myself for bed, there was a frantic banging on my door. Worried, I rushed to answer it and found Paul in the hallway, waving his phone and jumping from foot to foot.

'The Northern Lights are outside!' he shouted. 'You've got to take a look.'

I'd yet to see the effervescent show that sometimes swirls above this part of the world. I knew that people paid thousands to see the Northern Lights, even travelling as far away as Iceland and the Arctic Circle for the briefest glimpse. Now they were just beyond my window.

When I stepped outside, it was as if the universe had cracked open and a vast, psychedelic cloud was spilling across the sky. The Technicolour display pulsed and swirled from red to green to purple. There had been times on the NC500 when the silence was so smothering that I'd heard the mechanics of my own body at work. My stomach flexed and twanged. My lungs swelled and deflated with the slightest of creaks. I heard my ligaments and joints clicking and snapping quietly. In the deathly quiet of the night sky, a weird energy vibrated around me. I could almost detect the electromagnetic charge of the galaxy. It felt like a religious experience.

I stood and watched for hours.

* * *

I was enjoying my newfound power, free of the opinions of others, and dreaming of a life where I could exist happily by living on The Path every day. *Maybe the idea of becoming a walking ambassador wasn't so out of reach?* It was certainly validating whenever someone contacted me online or approached me on the trails with the intention of taking a challenging journey of their own. Now, two years on from my own fateful decision, the notion of being a trekking figurehead didn't seem so unrealistic, not like it had done when I'd first mentioned it to my brother as we sat in his car, staring at the sea, the rain hammering down outside. Back then, I'd been cut short by pragmatic thinking. Suddenly, the plan felt tangible and within reach.

The daily walks continued and I marched around the coastline past Bettyhill and Thurso, before arriving at John O'Groats – the yin to Land's End's yan, and the finish line (or starting point) to so many charity walks. I posed by the famous wooden sign that arrowed towards Shetland in one direction (152 miles) and New York the other (3230 miles). I gawped at the Duncansby Stacks, the huge triangular rock formations that emerged, like supersized shark's teeth, from the North Sea. Then I sank pints with a group of geologists from Kent, who educated me on the processes responsible for creating the region's mind-bending landmarks. I felt totally at home. Everything was in its right place.

Then November arrived and winter smashed into me like a Jonah Lomu rugby tackle. The nights shortened, the rain became heavier, and my breath fogged in the air in thick plumes. On some evenings, as I rested in Paul's living room after a solid day of walking, it took ages for my bones to warm up. The damp had seeped into the deepest nooks of my muscles and ligaments. My dirty clothes smelled like the inside of a hamster cage. Winter in Scotland was no joke and the darkness was unsettling. On some days, the sun didn't appear until eight in the morning, then it disappeared at three in the afternoon. For most of the day, I relied on my headtorch to light the trail ahead and I sensed my body weakening in the bad weather.

Once I'd eventually reached the end of my time on the NC500 after five weeks of walking, I said a sad farewell to Paul at Inverness. But we weren't to be separated for long. A few weeks later, once I'd reached Dundee – pushing past Elgin, Peterhead and Aberdeen at a fair pace – and settled down in a city hotel for the night, he called. Apparently, his car required an MOT, and given Stoer's remoteness, Dundee was the closest town with a suitable garage. *Would I like to meet for a coffee?* I gave him a time and location, and the following morning, as we sat in a nearby café, Paul explained how his car was knackered, while I complained about my broken body, which was suffering in the plummeting temperatures. Eventually, he made a suggestion.

'I've can't collect my car until next week,' he said, 'That means I've got to come back here. Why don't you come to Stoer for a break? You can recover for a bit and I can drop you in Dundee when I come back . . .'

I looked at the calendar on my phone. I hadn't yet made any sleeping arrangements for the foreseeable future. So, feeling a huge sense of relief, I nodded enthusiastically.

'Mate, I'd love to,' I said.

Several hours later, I was sat in his living room as the pair of us watched telly and thawed out in front of the fire. I was in heaven, relaxed, and entirely at home, and for several days I remained glued to the sofa, my taut muscles and ligaments finally softening and releasing, until one night, as I stretched on the floor, my right knee unexpectedly clenched. Whenever I bent my leg, there was an unsettling snagging sensation in the ligaments around the cap, as if something had caught on a displaced bone. It hurt like hell. The sound, a watery, jagged *pop*, only added to the feeling that something very wrong had happened.

The next afternoon, as a community doctor hinged and flexed my leg and felt around the muscles in my calves and quads, I heard a series of worrying sighs and tuts. Apparently,

I'd overdone it and strained my IT band, the connective tissue in each leg that runs from a person's glutes to their kneecaps. The one in my right side had pulled tight and the pain was presenting in my knee, which explained the nauseating snagging sensation. Then the doctor delivered an upsetting recovery plan:

'If you don't rest for six to eight weeks, you'll probably end up in surgery.'

I looked at my calendar. *Shit*. Resting now would mean losing a lot of ground.

The doctor listened to my story and picked up on my anxiety. 'Do you have some-where to stay?' he said. 'Wild camping with that type of injury isn't advisable. Especially in this weather.'

I nodded. 'Yeah, I think so,' I said, knowing that Paul wouldn't mind if I crashed at his for a while.

There was another exciting incentive to rest in one spot. The 2022 World Cup, the first to be held in December, was just about to start. For the next month, as Paul fussed about me, football was life. I stared at the big screen and stuffed my face with biscuits, while telling myself that the extra pounds around my waist would insulate me from the cold when I next hit The Path.

After a month or so, the popping in my knee was reduced to a soft click and I tested my strength with a short walk along the nearby trail. The rain had thickened to snow, everything was white, and as the icy cold bit into my ears, nose and cheeks, I wondered if I should wait a few weeks more. Then the whispering of The Path returned. I pulled up my collar and called upon my now impervious self-belief. I walked for two kilometres. The next day I managed three. Then four. Then five.

There were one or two setbacks along the way – on one walk, Paul had to drive me home when my knee tightened painfully. But a fortnight later, I was racking up 30 kilometres yomps in the shin-deep drifts.

After nearly two months on the mend, I was fit and rested and mulling over what was now within my grasp. Once I'd rejoined The Path in Dundee, I would have to battle with the jagged northwest coastline around St Andrews and Kirkcaldy, and then Edinburgh and Eyemouth. But once across the border I only had the east and southern coastlines of England to go – a route that was comparatively flatter than Scotland and I wanted to see how quickly I could go. Trekking around Scotland had created a satisfying equilibrium, where I was able to savour my time on the trails and feel so in the moment that the physical and emotional grind required to push forwards became second nature. A football manager or sports coach would have described me as being 'in the zone'. The sensation was exhilarating and satisfying. But I had my eye on the bigger prize.

The finish line.

Something significant had happened. During those recovery weeks, I'd started pondering the idea of doing a second lap. The concept was loose at first. I had no real strategy for how to manage it, or when I might commit to spending another chunk of time walking the British coastline, but a mission plan was brewing. I'd been left frustrated at how Covid had punctuated my progress at the start of 2021, particularly when I'd left Nicola and David's to work with Simon in Portscatho. Months had been lost. When I'd first set out on my journey, the initial hope had been to complete the loop in around a year, and I was now well off track. But time had become a teacher and my growth since those early days of walking, when I'd been naïve to the realities of homelessness, was now obvious. It had convinced me that I could walk The Path in a much quicker time.

When I mentioned the idea to Paul, he asked if I'd lost the plot. 'Why the hell would you want to do it a second time?' he said eventually.

'I don't know,' I said. 'Because it's an itch? Because I want to prove to myself that it can be done? I've met so many nice people in doing this. I want to be able to come back and stay with all the new mums and dads I've found. Like you. . .'

He laughed. 'Well, you can come back whenever you want. But maybe finish the first lap before committing to another? You don't have to prove anything to anyone.'

Yeah. Maybe. 'I'm sure it's the former Marine in me that wants to go even harder,' I said. 'Or do it better.'

Heeding Paul's advice, I decided to sit with the plan for a week or two, instead of announcing a second loop online (and placing a whole load unnecessary pressure on myself). And yet the fantasy was becoming unshakeable. I felt dialled in, and during my last few recovery walks, I was reminded of those training exercises as a Marine when my unit had stepped into enemy territory. Faced with a daunting challenge, I would tune out all distractions. My muscles became ready for action; my mind told me anything and everything was possible. And it had been *otherworldly*. I experienced the same feeling when I visualised myself on The Path for a second time.

When I eventually left Paul in Dundee in February, saying farewell was emotional. As with Nicola and David, I left his company knowing I'd grown as a human. His kind nature, support and wisdom had been inspiring. But I was now more determined than ever to move on at speed. As his support wagon disappeared into the distance for the last time, I felt the familiar lurch of sadness. I hated saying goodbye. But rather than burying my feelings, I acknowledged their presence and reframed the hurt. 'The sadness was an indicator of good times spent with good people,' I told myself. Grief was the equal and opposite reaction to love. And there was so much of it in my new existence that the pain of saying farewell had become a regular occurrence.

Shortly afterwards, my phone vibrated with a text:

@Paul: *PS. If you ever decide to turn gay, do let me know.*

A winking emoji appeared, just in case I thought he was being serious.

I laughed and typed back:

@Warrior Walker: *Thank you, bro. Really kind of you to offer. It's not happening. But you keep dreaming.*

Then I carried on down the trail, knowing I'd made yet another new best friend.

CHAPTER FIFTEEN

BATTLE-SCARRED

Once beyond Dundee, I made steady progress. My knee injury became a distant memory and as the trail turned me towards Newport-on-Tay and the North Sea, I felt more excited about my progress. Looking at the map, there wasn't a lot of mileage or months between my current position and the finish line in Dorset. The realisation that my journey was very nearly done flooded my system with euphoria. My bootsteps were spring-heeled and determined. Winter was turning into spring, a new season was coming and, having vocalised my new ambitions to Paul, I felt more determined to race for home. As far as I was concerned, the sooner I finished, the sooner I could start again.

I was in an almost meditative state and grounded by the crunch of sand and stone underfoot, the sea to my left, the wind spiralling around me. I looked happy, which I was. As had been the case on the West Highland Way, strangers often asked me about my relaxed state of mind. More than one dog walker told me I appeared to be at peace. These observations amplified the good vibes in what was becoming a positive, emotional feedback loop. When the rain hammered down, it pushed me forward. If I connected with another walker on The Path, it encouraged me to cement a new friendship. And after I'd retold my story, I made sure to find out about the person on the other side of the conversation. All of us were living a fascinating narrative, whether we knew it or not. I now wanted to dive into those stories too.

This attitude helped me to become fluent in human, and I was arriving at every new meeting with an empathetic attitude, one that hadn't been available to me before because I'd been so closed off by my own shitty problems. But recently, the issues from my old life had become battle scars and I wore them like tattoos, as if they were nothing more than reminders. They represented a learned lesson or two, rather than a series of life-threatening emotional injuries, and they allowed me to understand the pain of others. Whenever someone approached me for a chat, I knew quite quickly if they were sad or lonely, angry or grieving, often before they'd opened their mouths to speak. Rather than only processing my own pain, I'd found the room to listen and feel as people expressed theirs.

This shift had become apparent after I'd stayed with a bloke who owned a coffee shop somewhere close to the NC500. (I don't want to name him because I'm not sure if his story has been told beyond an immediate circle of friends, so I'll refer to him as the Coffee Shop Owner from now on.) His life was basic; luxuries and frills weren't his thing, and his stripped-back store emitted a soothing atmosphere of tranquillity. I'd felt calmed as soon as I stepped inside and heard the tinkling door chimes. The smell of cinnamon and scorched coffee grounds tickled my nostrils. Everything was peaceful. When we talked, I learned he'd lived in Japan for 20 years and the design ethic of his store was heavily influenced by their culture: we sipped coffee from small cups, dinner was a delicious bowl of ramen and I slept on a futon. Everything was chill and Zen-like.

But the Coffee Shop Owner's backstory seemed tinged with regret. Having moved back to the UK, he'd found himself in a weird place, but a newfound faith in God kept him steady. He'd dedicated himself to the simple life and served coffee, keeping his expenses to a minimum and doing his best to help others. 'I've never wanted money,' he told me over dinner. 'I don't want a social media profile. I just want to pray and help people. And I do that through coffee.' It was an attitude I could get with; it's how he'd connected with me, after all.

But there was a sadness to the Coffee Shop Owner. Something wasn't quite right and whenever our conversations deepened or became emotional, he withdrew, as Paul had done. I let him be because it was his story to tell, not mine to push for, but I guessed he was carrying a lot of pain. I recognised the emotional frequencies from the time when my own life was screwed up and I'd been closed off.

This understanding was an important step forward, but it would have been wrong to think I was fully fixed or qualified to fix the hurt in others. The demons were still close by, and every now and then, I heard them whispering to me through a familiar inner dialogue. But The Path had given me the tools to cope. Whenever I experienced a moment of sadness, maybe when considering the Allied forces' withdrawal from Afghanistan, or while remembering a painful argument during my break-up with Joy, I used the hurt as propellant. Rather than succumbing to its weight, I distracted myself by playing a game. If another walker appeared on the horizon, I made it my mission to catch them, regardless of how far ahead they were. Likewise, if someone was closing in on me, I'd increase the pace until they became a speck in my rearview again. In my head, I was a champion marathon runner in a race where the only competitor was me.

And I made sure to win every day.

* * *

I was soon in Musselburgh, a town famous for being the largest in East Lothian and its Roman settlement, which was built after their invasion in 80 AD and the first settlement built by the Romans. Perched on the coast around eight kilometres from Edinburgh, it sat by the pretty River Esk and overlooked the Firth of Forth estuary, and the North Sea beyond. My host for the night was a posh bloke called Anthony, another random from the internet, and we'd connected through a series of social media messages and comments. From what I could tell, Anthony came from a family of landowners. A charitable type, he'd invested his money wisely and was also injecting his funds into a series of successful business ventures. These investments were now reaping serious rewards. All of which was a roundabout way of saying that Anthony was doing OK.

He owned a house just outside the town and had excitedly

invited me to stay for a few days. But when we spoke on the phone for the first time, I was a little taken aback. Anthony sounded like King Charles. This impression was furthered when he picked me up in his mud-splattered Toyota Hilux truck. Anthony resembled every posh bloke I'd ever seen on TV, and as all six foot three of him unfolded slowly from the car seat to greet me, I clocked the uniform of the wealthy and well-mannered. Luxury brand wellies, check. Scruffy trousers tucked inside, check. Oxford collar shirt, check. And, of course, a scuffed Barbour jacket. Sprouts of greying, curly hair were attempting to escape from the flat cap perched upon his head. Shaking my hand firmly, Anthony welcomed me with a cheery smile. He seemed bloody lovely.

'Now, Paul,' he said proudly, 'one must treat my home as if it were yours.'

He gestured for me to get into the truck as I tried to explain to him that I was a good house guest, very considerate and eager to wash my own underwear. But Anthony was having none of it.

'All very well and good,' he said, raising a hand. 'But as I said: *my house is yours.*'

During the journey through the backroads, Anthony gave me his story, a wildly entertaining tale that involved a sister (who worked for the Red Cross, or the UN, or some other very important institution, I wasn't quite sure) and his latest business excursion, which involved the distribution of air-conditioned tents. Everything sounded fantastical; potentially boring details were wrapped in an atmosphere of flamboyant derring-do. Anthony, by the sounds of it, had friends in high places, moved within the echelons of power, and his technology had gathered admiring glances from a series of supermarket chains. But currently, it was being used to shelter displaced communities in challenging climates.

'People?' I said, confused.

'Yes, people!' laughed Anthony. 'In Sudan, of all places, where they've been having a refugee crisis. The tents are now assisting the humanitarian effort over there.'

He chuckled, as if to suggest this mind-blowing achievement was all part of a day's work – which for him, it probably was. 'Anyway, like I said: you have the run of the place. Use the shower. Sleep whenever you want. Eat whatever you want from the fridge. I won't be gone long.'

Wait, what? 'Where are you going?' I said, feeling a little taken aback. Yet another person was leaving me in their home, alone, not really knowing too much about me.

'Ah, well, I've been offered a ticket to the rugby this afternoon. Scotland are playing in the Six Nations. It's part of a charity event . . .'

I shrugged. *Fair enough.* But Anthony's generosity was not to be the most surprising event of the afternoon. After several minutes spent bouncing along a wide country lane, the throughfare opened out into a grand courtyard. At the far end was the type of manor house that wouldn't have looked out of place in *Downton Abbey.* My jaw drooped. I'd never seen so many windows on a house before. A wide flight of stairs, framed by pillars, led up to a huge front door. I wondered if a butler was about to emerge with a silver platter holding overflowing champagne flutes.

'Bloody hell, mate,' I said, stunned. 'You live here?'

Anthony stopped the car and unfolded himself from the seat again. 'Well, yes. As do you for a few days.'

When we stepped inside, I wasn't sure what to do with myself. Dressed in old kit, still stinky from full day of walking, I felt completely awkward in a home that had, quite likely, seen one or two royals walking the halls. Whenever I went to London, I made sure to visit the Tate Britain gallery. Its permanent collection featured paintings by JMW Turner, John Singer Sargent and John Everett Millais. Some of the art pieces hanging from Anthony's walls would have sat quite nicely in its world-famous collection. I had to stop myself from gawping as he showed me through the house, pointing out the various living rooms, bedrooms (of which there were many) and bathrooms (ditto). It was like walking through a plush hotel, the type you might see in an Agatha Christie whodunnit.

The surprises didn't end there. When I then asked to use the toilet, I was shocked to see a familiar-looking briefcase on the floor. Made from a blood red leather and decorated with angular, metal-tipped corners, it was topped with a heavy silver handle. On the front was an instantly recognisable gold logo. A crown perched on top of the letters ER II. I froze. *Fucking hell.* It was the regal emblem of the late Queen. *Is Anthony a royal?* Then I remembered: I had seen this briefcase before, or one very similar to it, every autumn when the Chancellor of the Exchequer departed Downing Street to deliver his or her annual budget. It signalled the time of year when people learned the price of an average pint and moaned about their income tax rates. I left the toilet with the distinct impression I was now flying at a political altitude that was beyond my comprehension.

'Er, Anthony,' I shouted, as he busied himself on a laptop in the kitchen. 'What's with the briefcase in your loo?'

But he was still typing furiously. I wondered if he might be corresponding with the prime minister of a boiling hot country, one in desperate need of an air-conditioned tent.

'Ah yes,' he said, almost absently-mindedly. 'My father was in Parliament. The briefcase was given to him as part of the job.'

I felt muddled. But before I could press Anthony for more details, he closed his computer and started gathering his things. 'Anyway, I'm terribly sorry but I have to leave now.'

'Already?' I said, following him through the hallway. 'What should I do?'

Anthony was pulling on his jacket. He gestured to the fittings and fixtures of a home I couldn't have imagined crashing in. 'Enjoy the place,' he said. 'The kitchen is down the hall, so help yourself to beers. I'll bring dinner back for us. But really, just put your feet up and relax, Paul. You've bloody well earned it.'

But I couldn't relax. I felt on edge. Anthony's place was too nice, too grand and too expensively decorated for me to feel anything other than nervous, especially when resting my dirty socks or grubby hands on any opulent-looking furniture. When I later walked the corridors towards the kitchen, I assessed every step carefully, making sure to stay clear of the vases and ornaments lining the walls. It was like stepping into a living episode of *Antiques Roadshow*. To overcome my anxiety, I focused on feeling a sense of gratitude for Anthony's incredible generosity.

This is cool, bro, I told myself. *I've gone from sleeping in hedges, church doorways and a barn with a rat and a load of cows to being given the run of a manor house. This is a bit of me. I'm welcome here.*

I stepped into the kitchen, only to have my illusions shattered instantly. At the other end of the vast room was a giant labrador. It had reared up in its basket and was growling loudly. Flecks of spittle dripped from an impressive set of fangs. I took a deep breath. The Path had introduced me to hundreds of dogs; I was well-versed in the type of behaviour required to calm an anxious pet. But as I took a slow step into the kitchen, the beast charged at me, barking aggressively. Realising I was out of my depth, I took an instinctive step backwards and managed to slip through the door. No way was I being used as a chew toy. Closing it behind me, I heard the dog growling on the other side. Then I edged fearfully down the corridor, taking care not to knock anything of value to the ground, wondering if I might have been better off sleeping in a barn.

CHAPTER SIXTEEN

ME VERSUS ME

I stayed in the big house for two days feeling bewildered at yet another jammy hand dished out by fate. Anthony and his girlfriend were the perfect hosts, and as the three of us ate good food and told big stories, I tried to imagine a situation in which our lives might have connected ordinarily, but I really couldn't think of one. Anthony moved in an world populated by royalty and politicians. I was technically homeless and unlikely to become a multi-millionaire any time soon, so there was no chance we'd have met without me walking The Path and posting about it on social media. That didn't make us opposites, though. Despite the obvious differences, we found common ground in our shared love of sport, adventure and nature. And like so many other people I'd stayed with, Anthony bought into the idea that anyone could change their lives with a wild plan.

I sometimes wondered if my journey carried a sense of

romance for the people I was meeting, especially if they'd been feeling weighed down by responsibility, stress or financial pressure. Despite its obvious pain and anxieties, I had freedom on The Path and my journey showed that risk brought its own set of rewards – some of them obvious, others not so much. I was also living proof that anyone could change their lives. But despite the acts of kindness that were keeping me on track, I never felt like a charity case or a burden. It was quite the opposite, in fact. Sometimes it appeared that the sleepovers, sandwiches and coffees, while incredibly kind gestures, were benefiting the other person as much as me. The need for companionship, an inquisitive nature and sheer bloody boredom were powerful motivators, and I made sure to engage fully with anyone who offered me a helping hand.

There's a theory, after all, which suggests that every act of kindness benefits three people: the giver, the receiver and the observer. Whenever I stayed with someone, the giver often wanted to hear my stories and ask questions. I made sure to answer them all. As the receiver, I then tried to express gratitude, respect and admiration to the individual or family helping me out, because, in some cases, their assistance had been life-changing. When the experience was then retold on social media, the observer – anyone following my Instagram account – could create a narrative of their own. Some people laughed at my encounters. Others found inspiration or consolation. I really hoped that people with mental health issues were finding a little encouragement in my healing journey.

Because there was a way out, no matter how dark the circumstances.

After staying with Anthony, I booted through the rest of Scotland in three weeks and entered England, via Northumberland, with a point to prove to both myself and everyone following me. I realised that the route ahead of me was fairly flat, so I set myself a target of smashing through the lot in ten weeks. If it broke me, I was OK with it. I wanted to push myself to the limits by crossing the finish line a limping, sweating mess, the physical state celebrated by the famous Hunter S Thompson quote that stated: 'Life should not be a journey to the grave with the intention of arriving safely in a pretty and well-preserved body, but rather to skid in broadside in a cloud of smoke, thoroughly used up, totally worn out, and loudly proclaiming "Wow! What a Ride!"'

Yeah. *That.*

Even though I'd been fantasising about a second go around, the understanding that my journey was very nearly over felt destabilising. I hadn't been home since the summer of 2020, nearly three years previously, and the world had been so very different back then. *I* was so very different back then. To a lot of people I knew, I'd probably seem unrecognisable now, especially physically, having dropped a ton of weight since those dark, depressed days when I'd worked a nine-to-five office job. Mentally, I was drastically altered too, and I was interested to see how people were going to view the new me, especially Tommy and maybe even Dad. (Though he hadn't contacted me in all the time I'd been away, other than to wish me a happy Christmas or a happy birthday.) But another part of me worried about what might have shifted in my absence, both in the characters I'd known and the places I'd existed in.

Not all growth phases were painless, but they were usually worth it.

Before The Path, I'd considered myself a screw-up in life, love, career – just about everything. Shoulder-barged into the shadows by fate, I'd struggled silently in an emotional darkness. I found it hard to shake the sense that I was an ugly duckling, a waste of space and entirely unlovable. Thankfully, that turned out to be total rubbish.

In fact, my pain was the norm. Most people have periods of doubt, insecurity and anxiety because all three are part of the Human Experience. When I'd told myself that I couldn't do something or that I was destined for failure – that my hopes and ambitions were pointless or unrealistic – it was easy to feel alone in that doomy mindset because very few people around me were talking about their own failures. But over the past three years, a surprising, universal response had been beamed back at me. *Everyone experienced those same negative emotions.* Self-doubt and insecurity were facets of everyday life. Fear, disappointment and failure were obstacles that tested the most capable of individuals, regardless of age, gender or background. Being knocked down by an unfortunate event or a bad decision wasn't what defined us. Our responses did, and they remained very much within our power.

Everyone experienced struggle.

Everyone experienced heartbreak.

Everyone experienced missed opportunities and false dawns.

And everyone at some point reached a crossroads in life and turned one way, only to wonder what might have happened had they travelled in another direction.

Julian's words at the Temple Café suddenly felt more prescient than ever before. Say good things. Do good things. Believe good things. *Turn ripples into waves*. Just repeating what was a simple mantra became a reclamation of personal power. Meanwhile, every positive or reaffirming DM and comment on social media boosted my confidence. The collective feeling acted like a superhero cape, one I could use for everything I did going forward – the next coffee shop, the next encounter on The Path, the next moment of adversity.

Had I cracked the code? I wasn't entirely sure but from what I could tell, the only difference between those that *did* in life and those that *didn't* was self-belief. World history was littered with the bodies of talented individuals who failed to make their mark or achieve their ambitions because of doubt – the little voice that said 'nope'. Meanwhile, other, less talented individuals made it to the top because their internal voice was louder, and bolshier. Without creeping into arrogance or delusion, I wondered whether I'd found an inner cheerleader.

Meanwhile, The Path had revealed a flicker of light at the end of a bloody long tunnel. Characters like Anthony had shown me that there was a nice world out there with nice people, and I only had to step beyond my front door (wherever that might be) to connect with them. No one was perfect of course, but so many of us were doing our best. Simply arriving at that understanding helped me to accept the less-than-ideal situations in my world. Like my relationship with Dad: it wasn't me, *it was his circumstances,* and that was OK. When it came to Mum . . . well, I wasn't there yet. Our connection was still lost and occasionally I'd experience a pang of guilt because I wanted to find the right amount of forgiveness so badly, especially given the other, undeniable forward steps that had taken place. But that process would need a little more time.

I reassured myself that everything was OK, that it might happen one day, just not today, and made sure to remember something Nan had taught me when I was a little kid. One morning when I'd felt totally crushed, having been abandoned by my parents yet again, I'd sobbed loudly into her shoulder. Trying to console me, she suggested a way forward:

'You know, you can't choose your family, but you can build your own.'

That theory had only chimed with me 25 years later, as I yomped around Great Britain. Building a family, all of them friends from The Path, was my new thing. And by the looks of things, I was doing a pretty good job of it.

* * *

I was so attuned to the physical exertions of The Path that I was smashing out 15 successive days without resting. On some mornings, I'd wake early and walk for 50 kilometres. The distances bounced off me. The pressures that had once accompanied my early days in the walk, when I'd had nowhere to stay, were a distant memory. The weeks flew by as I moved down the northeast, then around Anglia and Essex, and across the Kent coast, where I was invited to stay with Julian and Emma, a couple I'd met in Margate. Summer was approaching. Everything was changing. The light, heat and a warm sea breeze brought a mood of new opportunities, and I drew on every drop of it. As we sat at the dinner table, Emma asked me if I'd like a reading.

'A reading?'

She smiled. 'Yeah, a tarot reading. I do them. But no pressure, only if you want to.'

Emma was very in touch with her spiritual side. There was a yoga room in her house. A set of sound bowls had been set up around the fireplace. Something about the energy in her home made me wonder if she was white witch or a mystic. I took up the offer and watched as she laid out a formation of cards on the table. Emma then turned them over one by one and detailed their meaning. With each explanation, my mind was blown. Everything had a story attached and every story resonated with my experience on The Path in some way. When the final card was revealed, adrenaline flooded my nervous system. It was an illustrated character holding a bow, and his arms and face were marked with tattoos – bright blue, ornate lines that curved across his skin. But it was his headwear that caused my flesh to goosebump. Sprouting from his skull was a set of gnarled antlers. *A stag*.

'No way!' I said.

Emma looked at me knowingly. 'This has some connection to you?'

'Well, yeah,' I laughed. 'Stags . . . I've been seeing them everywhere.'

I told the story of my first night on the path: the foxhole, my fright at being interrupted and my fitful sleep on the church steps. According to Emma, this card was the Hunter and a sentence was printed on the bottom: 'Track down your fears and desires'. Apparently, it represented the Celtic god, Cernunnos, the stag god of the wild. Its energy was supposedly both fearful and fearless. As Emma read from the card, the hairs on the back of my neck stood up.

'Instead of being hunted down by your fears or other feelings that you might have buried, become the Hunter,' she said. 'You are being given confidence and strength at this time, so use your power to make a difference. You are not here to cower away or to live in the shadows. You are here to realise your fullest potential. But this can only occur when you step up and do what needs to be done.'

I laughed. 'Are you sure you're not pulling these cards out for my benefit?'

Emma shook her head. 'The deck never plays games,' she said seriously.

* * *

There were still moments when my inner cheerleader was challenged.

As I made my way towards Portsmouth one morning, over a gnarly path filled with ankle-breaking divots, I decided on a whim to make an excursion to the Isle of Wight. My island hop lasted just one day and when I checked a timetable for the ferries that crossed the Solent back to the mainland, starting from Yarmouth on the Isle of Wight's west coast and landing at Lymington in Hampshire, there was not a lot of time until the next one. To make it, I would have to run the rest of the way.

This is going to be close, I thought, tightening the straps on my Bergen.

Staying steady on the uneven terrain, I broke into a light jog, not stopping until I'd reached the port. But it hadn't been enough. The Wightlink ferry was pulling away. *Bloody hell. I'd nearly made it.* Panting, exhausted, I dropped my bag and slumped to the floor. *What a downer.*

For the first time in months, I felt a little defeated and experienced a brief moment of self-doubt, even though I was so close to the end. The superhero cape around my neck lost its power, as if this minor setback had been a brick of Kryptonite and I realised that I'd been on such a roll, knocking down the kilometres and coastal landmarks like skittles as I passed them by at speed, that anything other than progress now felt like a failure. I checked into Instagram and uploaded a status report. *I'm feeling sorry for myself,* I reported. The encouragement from my online support network, a barrage of uplifting messages, strongarm emojis, and you've-got-this love hearts, was instantaneous and empowering.

Not long to go now, Warrior . . .

Don't give up!

We've been following you for years. Don't stop. You're so close.

It wasn't long before I was able to course correct. I hadn't felt down because *I'd* failed. It was because I'd been thwarted by something beyond my control, in this case a ferry timetable, and being helpless was what frightened me most of all. I knew that it was within my power to complete a full loop of Great Britain and then go again. But my real fear throughout the walk had been that some outside factor would stop me, like an act of God, a financial incident or personal disaster.

I leaned into my Royal Marines training, reminded myself that I could only control the controllables and pressed ahead. After all, the incident had only put me a couple of hours behind schedule. Given I'd already been walking for three years, it was a hiccup I could live with.

* * *

When I eventually disembarked the Wightlink back in Lymington hours later, just 30 kilometres, give or take, separated me from a once unimaginable achievement. I checked my watch. The time was 7.00pm. If I was to finish my full loop of the British coastline that night, I had five hours to do so.

Then I heard a shout. 'Paul! The Warrior Walker?'

I turned around and noticed a bloke in the distance, waving. Staring, squinting, I realised it was someone I hadn't seen before. Sat beside him was a husky. It was calm and attentive, and looked more like a wolf than a dog. The stranger shook my hand and introduced himself as Stu. His furry mate, he explained, was named Skye, which felt like a huge coincidence, given my experiences in Scotland.

'Hello, bro,' I said, laughing. 'How's it going?'

'Pretty good, thanks. Listen. . . I've been following you for a couple of years online,' said Stu. 'I saw your story at the ferry port earlier, realised you were in a bad way and thought I'd drive down to help you on the last stretch.'

'Drive? Where have you come in from?'

Stu smiled. 'Not too far. . .' He looked sheepish. 'So . . .'

'So . . . ?'

'So, can I walk with you?'

'Yeah, sure,' I laughed. 'I'm going all the way to Mudeford tonight though, and it'll be at quite a clip. Can you keep up?'

Stu nodded and the pair of us, plus Skye, began striding along the promenade with the aim of making it past Keyhaven and Milford-on-Sea, around the beaches in Highcliffe, before ending the walk in Mudeford and finishing my mission in Sandbanks. But we couldn't have made it 100 metres when another man walked towards us purposefully. I'd become so accustomed to people approaching me on The Path that I knew he was waiting to meet me. His body language was a dead giveaway. As he got closer, I noticed he was smiling.

'Bloody hell, it is you,' he shouted, hugging me, before shaking Stu's hand awkwardly and scruffling Skye's fur. 'I wasn't sure I'd find you.'

'Mate, who are you?' I said, totally unsurprised at the encounter, but eager to keep walking.

'Joey,' he said, rummaging around in his coat for a bag of Fruit Pastels. 'Here, I bought you these.'

He opened the packet, took one for himself and shoved the rest into my pocket. 'Oh, and I've got this for you too.' Joey was waving a 20-quid note.

I shook my head. 'You don't have to—'

'Yeah, I know, but I saw your Instagram page a while back and it just . . . resonated.'

'What do you mean?'

The way Joey glanced down at the ground was a tell. He had a story.

'I've had some problems. I've been a mess, you know . . .

mentally.' Then his face lit up. 'Watching your videos really helped, though. The way you talk. *I got it.*'

Joey looked at me nervously. 'Can I walk with you for a bit?'

'Sure.'

Then he looked at Stu. 'Do you two know each other?' he said. 'I'm not interrupting anything, am I?'

'Never met him before in my life,' I said, reaching into my pocket for a Fruit Pastel. I needed the sugar.

Within five minutes, my aim of building a serious head of steam had taken yet another dent when a third man appeared. He was walking on the opposite side of the road and waving.

'Warrior Walker?' he said, excitedly.

You have got to be kidding me. 'Yeah? Do I know you?'

The man shook his head. 'No. Well, not properly. I'm Nick. We've spoken a few times on Instagram.'

Bloody hell. 'Really?'

I looked at Nick. Then at Joey. And finally at Stu. *Was this a wind up?* 'This feels like a wind up . . .'

Nick looked embarrassed. 'Well, I live an hour or so away and when I saw you were in the area, I had to come along.'

He nodded at Stu. Then he nodded at Joey. 'Is this a group thing, though? I don't want to get in the way. . .'

I smiled. 'Mate, you're totally fine. We're having a party.'

I looked around, hoping I'd gathered my final companion for the night. 'Come on, let's go.'

We walked towards Mudeford, chatting, telling stories. Stu was a personal trainer. Joey served in the army. Nick worked for a railway company in Southampton. All of us were complete strangers, none of us had ever met before in real life, and yet here we were, an oddball foursome – well, five if you included Skye – clocking up the final kilometres on a near three-year journey that had taken me around the British coastline. The moment reminded me of a famous scene from the movie *Rocky*: Sly Stallone running through the city of Philadelphia during a final training session ahead of his heavyweight showdown with Apollo Creed. As Rocky jogs through a street market, trailed by a mob of kids, someone throws him some fruit. He waves and takes a bite. The onscreen camaraderie is energising. It feels inspirational. And this was just the same.

I shoved another Fruit Pastel into my mouth.

'My wife thinks I'm nuts,' said Nick eventually. 'She was like, "Hanging about to meet a stranger. A hiker. *What's wrong with you?*"'

'And what did you say to that?'

'I told her: But it's the Warrior Walker. He's not a stranger. Like, he's just mad, you know?' Nick looked awkward again. 'Sorry.'

'Don't worry, mate,' I said, trying to put his mind at rest. 'I've heard worse.'

It felt good to have a team around me. Throughout the experience, I'd been championed by an army of online followers but they were voices in the ether – a valuable but intangible support team. The arrival of Stu, Joey and Nick had transformed my online network into something more tactile for the final kilometres, while to them, I'd become a 4D version of my online self. I told them about my adventures so far. The stag. The old lady. Nicola and David. Gareth's support car. The midges. Nan's locket. The idea of ripples into waves.

So much of it seemed to have happened a lifetime ago. I couldn't get my head around the fact that I was so near to the finish line. I thought back to Dad's scepticism as I'd struggled out of his front door, weighed down by all those jumpers and bottles of shower gel. It felt good to be proving a few people wrong.

We walked into the pitch black. Night smothered us, the rain too. By 9.30, Joey and Nick had returned to their cars. Nick's wife was probably worried about him. Stu and Skye stayed with me until 11.30 as I became delirious with fatigue. Remembering my name felt weirdly challenging – the words seemed out of reach and shrouded in thick fog. My vision was blurry, and the ground ahead looked to be trembling, like a wobbling bridge in an earthquake. Stu fed me more sweets until my blood sugar levels stabilised. Once I was in solid shape, he also had to leave. I hugged him and thanked him for the support, promising to let him know once I'd finished for the night. Then I turned and faced the black sea. Across the water, the lights of Bournemouth twinkled seductively in the distance.

I was so close.

CHAPTER SEVENTEEN

WHAT NEXT? (WHO CARES?)

Alone, I walked on for a few kilometres towards a pre-paid rental caravan at Mudeford – a final altruistic gift from an internet stranger. I was exhausted. Half of me, the delirious half, didn't want to rest. The finish line at Sandbanks beach wasn't even a day's walk away. The other, more rational half had realised that there was little point in rushing. Tommy and my brother Jack were set to meet me in the morning – they would understand. David was also driving down from North Devon to see me, though Nicola, sadly, was staying at home. I buzzed at the thought of seeing the different strands of my new family, together, in the same place for the very first time. Everyone had so far been connected through storytelling and Instagram photos. They were disparate dots on a map and strangers in the Real World. Suddenly, those connections were being pulled together, though Dad wasn't going to be there to join them.

One of my brothers was running a marathon that same day and he'd decided to support him instead. The news, when I found out, had been a brief buzzkill, but I got over it quickly. *Same old, same old,* I thought.

I let myself into the caravan, kicked off my trail shoes and stretched out on the bed. The physical effort of the day's walk crushed me at once. My eyes fluttered and drooped, I felt a heaviness in my chest and when I next looked around the caravan, it was flooded with sunlight. I had slept, uninterrupted, for several hours.

Bloody hell, I thought. *I'm going to be late for my own party.*

Looking down, I noticed my grubby walking shorts and socks. Everything was mud-splattered and in dire need of a wash, and when I sniffed the fabric of my t-shirt, it stank. I'd worn these clothes for a couple of days straight, even my underwear, but reminding myself that the final day of the walk was for me and nobody else, I shrugged away any social embarrassment and swapped out my ripe-smelling socks for a box-fresh pair. It was last item of clean clothing left, a gift from a mate, and I'd deliberately saved them for the final few kilometres as a little slice of celebratory luxury.

'So, this is it,' I said, tying the laces on my trail shoes. 'I can't believe it's nearly done . . .' I looked at my watch. The date was 23 April, 2023.

Then I got my stomp on.

I'd love to give you a full breakdown of my emotional state as I walked to Christchurch and Southbourne and then the final ten kilometres to Sandbanks beach, but it's a fog. I posted Instagram messages as I approached the end point and alerted friends of my ETA at the finish line. I felt light, as if I were gliding along on a feeling of pride. 'I've done it,' I said into my phone, to everyone watching online. 'I've done it.'

How, I wasn't quite sure.

This was the endgame in an epic mental journey. For the entire yomp, I'd wondered where my limits might be and on some days, I'd almost invited a physical collapse, masochistically ticking off 50km walks, even when my calves or shoulders were tearing and cramping. I under-ate and became dehydrated, and over-ate and puked on the roadside. Whether this was a deliberate and subconscious attempt at self-sabotage, I'm not sure, but I enjoyed hunting myself down, while edging perilously close to a breaking point. Then, having approached a potentially devastating crash, I somehow pushed on for one more step, another kilometre, the extra day. Rather than slowing down in those moments, I reimagined my fear as excitement and told myself a seductive lie. *I'm not scared,* I thought, *I'm excited.* This cheat code helped me to thrive during moments of stress or hurt, and I pushed ahead, every step taking me away from the darkest moment in my life, when I'd considered killing myself. The experience of completing a challenge that nobody believed I could finish had shown me that anything was possible.

The finish line was packed. I saw Tommy and his wife; David had arrived; my brother, Jack and his partner too. But there were lots of faces I didn't recognise, strangers who had followed me on Instagram or heard about me in the news. Two bootnecks, Richie and Cosmin, inspired by my story, had even turned up to say hello, even though I'd never spoken to them online or off. Some of them had brought their friends, family and workmates along, to say hello to a person that they had never met before. It was all so weird and the comedown was instantaneous. After feeling briefly overwhelmed, I became weirdly underwhelmed. Partly because I was so exhausted – I didn't have the capacity to absorb what was happening. But also because I suspected the job was only halfway done – as far as I was concerned, I still had another loop to go. Meanwhile, everyone wanted to press me about my plans for the rest of the year – some of them for the rest of my life – and I batted away the endless enquiries about my 'what next?' with a shrug. Who cared about the next job, the next home or the next career move?

'What about the now?' I remember saying to someone. 'The sun's shining. Everyone's happy. This feels like a nice moment to live in for a while . . .'

And then I was thanking everyone for coming and saying my farewells. I shook all the hands and enjoyed all the hugs. I waved the Union Jack flag that had been tied to my Bergen for the past few weeks and posed for selfies. But there was a hollowness to my actions. At times, I seemed above myself, observing my actions rather than experiencing them, as if it were an out-of-body experience. David, who had been watching nearby, noticed my disconnect and quietly pulled me to one side.

'What do you want to do, Paul?' he said. I sensed he was offering me an escape route.

'Now?'

'Yeah. Right now. Where do you want to go?'

The thought of going back to Dad's place filled me with dread. The house was empty and I'd be alone again, as if I were back at square one.

'Can I come with you?' I said finally, laughing. I was only half joking.

David smiled. 'To stay? Because you're more than welcome.'

'Yeah, if that's OK?' I said, hopefully.

'Of course it's OK.'

With a groan, he lifted the Bergen onto my shoulders. Then we ordered two takeaway coffees from the nearby Coast Café and drove to North Devon.

* * *

As I fell into the rhythms of family life at Nicola and David's, a weird headspace kicked in, where the highs of walking The Path became an almost unreachable memory. I struggled to remember the important names, landmarks and events from my journey, to the point where I wondered if any of it had actually happened. To overcome what was a strange feeling of emptiness, I reassured myself that this was the type of emotional comedown experienced by a person having completed an all-consuming challenge – like a runner finishing their first ever marathon, a scientist after making a breakthrough or a musician having recorded their debut album. In such circumstances, once the euphoria of success had faded away, an emptiness often moved in. I felt hollow; it was as if my brain had been scooped out and replaced with candy floss. My synapses were misfiring and nothing made sense.

I even debated delaying going again, though this was an understandable response to an uncomfortable situation. I was flat broke. The dwindling numbers in my bank account had only piled on the anxiety and, for a while, I even considered working for a year, maybe two, so that I could feel more financially secure during my next adventure. Living on the brink of homelessness again filled me with dread and in my weakest moments, I told myself that The Path could wait. That I could save some money and trek the British coastline without the existential stress of sleeping rough. Then I could afford better kit, nicer equipment and the occasional reward for a job well done.

Thankfully, I talked myself out of it. I was pressing ahead, and to hell with the financial headaches.

With hindsight, crashing at Nicola and David's house encouraged me to stay the course. I felt safe and loved, which allowed me to think and plan without pressure. It also helped that I was living in a very different world this time. When I'd previously stayed in North Devon, Covid had closed off the country. The streets were empty; the coffee shops were shut and everybody moved in a state of paranoia. Fast forward a couple of years and the environment was changed. People laughed and joked in the cafés without masks. I hugged old friends and shook hands with new ones. And the vibes surrounding me were overwhelmingly positive. In such an environment, I could plan from a position of opportunity rather than making my decisions while trapped in a fear-based mindset.

The first point of order in this new atmosphere was to recover. The Path had taken no prisoners and I'd been beaten up from top to bottom. During the first week of rest, my feet were painfully bruised. Both Achilles tendons felt caught on some unknown bone, and my calves had seemingly been pumped full of concrete and pebbledash. Whenever I walked in silence, my joints snapped, crackled and popped, and the most basic of bodily functions, like sneezing or going to the toilet, became agonising. At night, I often slept for ten hours and siestas became my go-to response to a big lunch. I felt like a 90-year-old.

Time and rest gave me plenty of time to think. Throughout May, I realised that walking a second lap of Britain probably seemed like a masochistic act to most people. After all, when Sir Edmund Hillary and Tenzing Norgay had scaled Mount Everest, their immediate response wasn't to climb it again in a repeat ascent. One and done, that was their approach, and my guess was that most walkers completing a challenge like mine would have had a similar attitude. Smiling at the record-breaking potential of a second loop, I decided to call the challenge 'the Victory Lap' and set about establishing a basic route, plus a timetable of places I wanted to be at certain times.

David, given his military background, lit up at the thought of several weeks of mission planning. 'You're going to need these,' he said one morning, dramatically spreading dozens of Ordnance Survey maps across the kitchen table. The space had been commandeered as our mission control, base camp and mess hall rolled into one.

'Bloody hell!' I laughed, rifling through the pile, looking for the most up-to-date editions. 'How many of these have you got?'

'More than enough,' he said, unfolding what he considered to be the best of the bunch. 'We're going to plan a foolproof itinerary.'

David's emphasis on the *we* gave me a warm, reassuring feeling. I suddenly understood his progression to the rank of army major. Attention to detail was his thing.

'We'll create a hard copy and write your schedule on it,' he continued, sitting down at the table. 'It'll be your back-up guide if you're away from 5G or Wi-Fi. Just don't get it wet . . . or drop it in enemy territory.'

Now he was taking the piss. But as we laughed and munched on biscuits, I plotted my course while setting out four non-negotiable conditions for the forthcoming mission.

#1 I was completing the loop in one year, because I knew it was doable, and London was my official start line. The first lap had begun in Poole, near to Dad's front door – not because it was a symbolic gesture but because it had been the most convenient location. At the time, I'd not had a pot to piss in, and travelling somewhere by train, just to begin walking, would have put a massive dent in my budget. For the Victory Lap, I wanted to start and finish with a bang. Besides, if I made my first and final steps outside Buckingham Palace, 10 Downing Street or Big Ben, a little stardust would be sprinkled on the journey.

#2 I had to be in Scotland by 1 August. *Why?* Because getting there any later would see me walking through the harshest environments on The Path during the coldest months of the year. I wrote down a timetable that had me reaching Dundee ASAP and John O'Groats by 4 September. I wanted to be in Ullapool for my birthday three weeks later and back into England – via the West Highland Way – by October. It was a tough ask, and I would need to get my stomp on, but the alternative was to go slow and run the risk of walking through the snow, ice and sleet at a time when I would be alone for long periods. The first lap had shown me that a Scottish winter was a dangerous adversary. It had to be avoided at all costs.

#3 The walk needed to take place in an anticlockwise direction. The sea had been on my left-hand side for almost three years. It was a constant companion and it kept me company when my thoughts turned dark. I was now intrigued to see what the walk would look like from a different vantage point, with the sea to my right and Britain's geographical landmarks to my left. I was a changed person. Life felt very different to when I'd walked from Bournemouth and back, via Cornwall, the Welsh coast, the north west, Scotland, Northumberland, Anglia, Kent and, finally, Hampshire. Taking a similar route, but in reverse order, was the perfect way to underline my new reality.

#4 I was raising money for charity. The kindness of strangers had got me through the past few years, and I had benefited greatly from Nicola and David's generosity, among others. As I'd yomped, strangers had offered me coffees, places to stay and new items of kit and clothing. People I hadn't met on The Path bought me drinks on a Go Fund Me page and booked hotel rooms so I could rest properly. I now wanted to repay the balance. I picked out several charities that meant something to me – The Samaritans, Doctors Without Borders, the Great North Air Ambulance, and MIND – with the intention of donating as much cash as I could through sponsorship. This was also a psychological hack. There were going to be moments on the Victory Lap when my motivation would be tested. Having a cause to work for would likely keep me on task.

As I established my start point, timeline and route with David, the challenge became a little more real. But with that realness came a flood of pressure. When I announced my new mission online, mates and family once again questioned my priorities, with the most common observation being that one lap was surely enough. *Why did I have to go for another?* I then heard suggestions that echoed Dad's traditional attitude. I was told that The Path wasn't real life. That I should think about getting a job, finding a new home and settling down. When I explained to people that my dream was to walk forever, in a commercially viable way, those ambitions were picked apart too.

'You need a business plan,' they said.

'You have to run a SWOT analysis first,' they said.

'You'll go broke in a couple of months,' they said.

No chance, I thought. *I found a way before. I'll find a way again.*

The biggest stresses were self-inflicted, though. Despite my bravado in announcing the Victory Lap, I still had doubts over my ability to complete the job within a self-imposed 12-month deadline. On one or two nights, I tossed and turned, fretting at some imagined moment in an undetermined future where I abandoned the walk. The thought of letting everyone down, and myself, made me nauseous, but rather than suffering in silence, I vented my fears to Nicola and David. They reassured me that anxiety was to be expected and that no amazing feats ever came without a level of fear, uncertainty or doubt.

'If they didn't, they wouldn't be considered amazing feats in the first place,' said Nicola reasonably.

I kept myself calm, looked at the Scottish border on the map and reminded myself of 1 August.

'Winter is coming,' I said, recalling a famous line from the TV show *Game of Thrones*.

Time to get a wriggle on.

CHAPTER EIGHTEEN

RED PILL/BLUE PILL

The itinerary for my first week on the Victory Lap was straightforward. After leaving London, I planned to follow the River Thames towards Essex, before turning north at Maldon, a name synonymous with the coastal town's famous salt. According to David's research, this route was the fastest line to England's east coast. After that, I 'only' had to walk up the map towards the Scottish border, but this approach was deliberately designed to create a feelgood factor. On the relatively flat trails of East Anglia and Norfolk, I'd likely make good ground; it was hoped that ticking off several northern counties in double-quick time afterwards would charge my self-belief to even higher levels. By the time I'd passed Newcastle and Berwick-upon-Tweed and stepped into Scotland, my body would be battle tested and physically ready for the more arduous parts of the walk.

At least, that's what David reckoned.

As I prepared, there was a methodical approach to everything

I did, which was so very different to my first departure in 2020. Back then, Dad had eyeballed me and my kit suspiciously, while I was nervous and unsure, feeling the fear and going ahead with it anyway. However, at Nicola and David's, the experience was entirely opposite. I thrummed with excitable energy as they both buzzed around me with encouraging and empowering words. My old kit bag also felt a world away: the heavy Bergen was replaced by a lightweight waterproof dry bag stuffed with the bare minimum: underwear, a bundle of socks, three or four t-shirts, some shorts, a rain jacket, a pair of waterproof trousers and a battered paperback book. I'd also packed a wash kit, headtorch and phone charger. Little sachets of electrolytes, flavoured powders that were great for preventing dehydration when mixed with water, were shoved into the corners. The whole lot couldn't have weighed more than 12kg.

This rig was of course not intended to keep me alive in the winter. Rather than playing Russian roulette with the elements, I intended to have some winter kit delivered to a friend's address in John O'Groats. When I arrived there, hopefully in September, I could switch it in time for the turning seasons.

I arrived in London on 5 June, where I carb-loaded on pizzas and did my best to get a good night's rest. My brain jangled with nervous energy. I couldn't wait to get started and when I set out from my starting point at Stratford tube station – where the headquarters for the mental health charity, MIND, were located nearby – the sensation of being back on The Path, yet in the capital, was entirely surreal. The sea felt a million miles away. I was disconnected from the coastal winds and the briny air.

Meanwhile, the human traffic – a mass of commuters swimming in the rush-hour currents – was headed in the opposite direction to me. They were racing towards the centre of London whereas I was very much leaving it, hopefully for a year.

The fact that I was pushing against the tide of workers seemed symbolic in some way and I was reminded of the sci-fi conspiracy movie *The Matrix Reloaded*. In one famous scene, the lead character, Neo (played by Keanu Reeves) finds himself faced with a crowd of people – all of them clones of his nemesis and all-round bad dude, Agent Smith. My situation felt eerily similar, though in this instance, the commuters that were pushing and shoving this way and that represented my insecurities and fears about the walk ahead. But as I began to stress, I used my emotional strength to bat them away, focusing on the facts and logic of my mission rather than feelings.

Have I gone too soon? No. I'm rested and mentally ready.

Is my body going to cope? Yes and no. But when the pain comes, I'll know how to react.

Can I do this? Of course! I did it once already and survived. There's no reason why I can't do it again.

And no one has done this twice. So this is my new purpose.

Muscle memory kicked in soon afterwards. With every step, I experienced the familiar push and flex in my legs, and I couldn't help but smile. My happy place had returned and it was showing – passersby eyed me suspiciously because I'd gone against the unwritten code of big city conduct, where visible scowls of misery and indifference acted like protective, but isolationist, forcefields. I honestly couldn't help it. I was back on the trail.

'This is what I do,' I said quietly, briefly imagining I was addressing the surging commuter rush as I cut through their moving mass.

'This is what I'm best at. And no one can beat me.'

Then I disappeared into the crowd, pushed to the other side, and took my first steps towards the sea.

* * *

As I walked along the Thames towards Maldon and Essex, everything was the same but different, and when I reached the coast a couple of days later, the sight of the water on my opposite side was as disorienting as I'd expected – like cleaning my teeth left-handed, rather than with my more dominant right. It took a few hours to adjust to the perspective shift, and to distract myself from the weirdness, I focused on the potential reunions that were due to take place during my second lap. Anthony in Musselburgh – that would be fun. Paul in Stoer – hopefully, we'd see the Northern Lights again. Mark, Julian and Amanda in the Temple Café – I couldn't wait to tell them about my experiences of turning ripples into waves. And that was just in the first few months. I'd even arranged to meet some of the people I'd once shared a desert island with on *Shipwrecked*. Back then, we'd camped under the stars on a remote beach. The experience would be totally different this time around.

I moved around the east coast, comfortably knocking out 45km and 50km days on the easy terrain, as David had suggested. The summer light warmed my face; the sea breeze kept me cool. My strides were strong and confident, and I was unbothered by the knee injury from earlier in the year. I booted it past

Felixstowe and up towards Lowestoft's esplanade, where I was confronted with the Statue of Triton – a stone representation of the famous sea god. Seeing old seafront monuments made me feel weirdly nostalgic, like a kid on a seaside holiday. I used to love messing around on the Poole waterfront during those seemingly eternal summers in the nineties.

In those days, six weeks away from school ushered in a feeling of freedom and opportunity. Every day was an adventure. I spent most of the time outdoors, and it was only once I'd got home in the evening that things took a turn for the worse. I was living with Mum, who was in her own headspace, and she sometimes dragged me to work at her catering business, which was a right downer. But when I was off the leash, the world felt safe and open, and I wanted to explore every bit of it. Without smartphone technology, I relied on the sun as my guide. I was out of the house once it hit a certain point in the sky, and then I'd play football, bomb around on my bike and cause mischief until it dipped beyond the horizon. I was young and my whole life was ahead of me. Everyone else was old and clueless to what a kid like me was all about.

It was all so very different now. I was turning 40 in the autumn of 2023, a landmark event, but the world around me seemed so much darker than it had been during my younger years. The coastlines of my youth were idyllic, all sandy beaches and rockpools wriggling with crabs or shrimps, and nearby cafés sold 99 Flake ice creams for 99p. The British seaside I was witnessing as a grown-up felt very different. The effects of global warming and pollution were impossible to ignore. The weather whiplashed between freakishly hot and wintery cold, even during the warmest months of the year. Meanwhile, plastic littered the beaches – it washed up as bottles, supermarket carrier bags, and discarded buckets and spades – and the industrial machine spewed smoke from furnaces and farted sewage into the sea. Seagulls feasted on landfill banquets and then washed up dead on the shore. I saw hundreds of them as I headed north.

My childhood summers, and the rose-tinted spectacles I viewed them through, seemed like a long time ago, in a galaxy far, far away. I really wished the world could go back there – and stay forever.

* * *

The fear of winter kept me glued to The Path. I had to be in Scotland by 1 August and my schedule nagged at me every day, tying me to a solid routine. After rising at 5am, I'd attempt to crank out as many kilometres as possible before the sun got too hot, and I enjoyed the determined grind because the morning was my favourite time of the day. It brimmed with optimism – before midday there was a new hope in everything I did and I felt excited that there were so many hours ahead of me. I thought about who I was going to meet, what dogs I was going to scruffle and the natural wonders I was likely to encounter. In the morning, I had direction and momentum. It was a powerful combination that made me believe that anything was possible. My future, while still uncertain, felt safe. On a good day, that idea stayed with me until I'd fallen into bed, knackered, usually around 11pm.

When walking for long periods along the British coast, there's an inconvenient reality that goes unmentioned in most

Ordnance Survey maps and tourist guides. Public toilets can be bloody hard to find, and those that are signposted have often been vandalised or abandoned in a state of disrepair by the local authorities. This was particularly troubling when drinking as much coffee as I did and eating 4,000 to 5,000 calories daily as a way of keeping the cardiovascular engine burning. As I walked, I feasted on bananas, berries, nuts and wholegrain carbs. I made sure to rehydrate with electrolytes and litres and litres of water. I refuelled like an athlete, rather than a Marine (as I had done during the first lap) and had learned to avoid big breakfasts, hearty lunches and sumptuous dinners. As a result, my fibre intake was high and my bowel movements were regular, sometimes painfully so.

My eagerness to stay hydrated meant I was caught short from time to time, which occasionally proved embarrassing. One morning, as I moved towards Northumberland, I overdid it on water and coffee. I felt the familiar knot in my bladder and desperately looked around for a toilet. With nowhere to go, and my midriff feeling as if the Xenomorph from the horror film, *Alien*, had taken up residence, I scanned the horizon for any incoming dog walkers or hikers. The trail behind me was empty but some way in the distance was a woman and her dog. Feeling certain they were far away enough, and not wanting to waste any precious time, or wet my pants, I stepped to the side of the track, unzipped and opened the floodgates. The relief was instantaneous. But after a 30 seconds or so, I heard a voice from behind me.

'Having a nice wee?' it said.

I finished as quickly as I could, and zipped up. When I turned around, I saw the woman and her dog. *Bloody hell, she got here quick.* Her spaniel was sniffing around in the grass. I froze in horror. *Please don't go there.* The woman quickly pulled out her lead as my face flushed with embarrassment.

'I'm so sorry,' I said, quickly sanitising my hands. 'I saw you all the way up there and thought I had time to finish.'

I rubbed my palms dry on my trousers. 'I'm Paul. You walk fast, by the way.'

'I have to with Bonnie,' said the woman, pointing to the dog, as she reached out to shake my hand. 'I'm Jane.'

She was eying up my rucksack. 'Off for a long walk?'

Well, sort of. I gave her my shortened pitch of how I came to walk The Path and why I was now doing a second lap. It only took a minute. My spiel was well-drilled.

She laughed. 'Wow, that's some story! Sounds like you're on a real adventure.'

I liked her. Jane seemed to have a kind energy, but her body language was off balance and telling a story that contradicted the smile on her face. Then her bottom lip trembled.

'I just knew it,' she said, looking up at the sky. 'I knew he would send me a Marine today . . .'

Uh-oh. 'He?' I said. 'What do you mean?'

Jane composed herself and dabbed at her eyes. She was doing her best not to cry. 'Joe, my son,' she laughed, wryly. 'I knew that if I needed someone today, he would send me a tall, strong Marine with a beard. Turns out I needed someone . . .'

She was really crying now. 'Do you need a hug?' I asked.

Jane nodded. I wrapped my arms around her and tried to calm her sobbing. 'Hey, it's OK. Do you want to talk about it?'

She pulled away and blew her nose loudly. 'I knew that my son would send me someone to do with the Marines. He was a naval officer.'

Shit. The past tense. I steeled myself.

'Before I saw you, I was at my son's memorial bench. We had one bench made for him and it's over there.' She was pointing to the hill where I'd first spotted her. It seemed a lot closer now than it did a few minutes ago. 'He passed away. Car accident.'

'I'm sorry.'

'It's OK, but thank you. He was coming home to see me. Joe took the same road he always did. He'd done it so many times, but this time . . . This time he came around the corner and an oncoming car hit him. Killed him. But his girlfriend survived. The first responder, an Air Ambulance guy, was an ex-Marine too and he kept Joe alive long enough so we could get there to say goodbye.'

I squeezed her tighter this time. No words could help in that moment. The story had wiped me out; I couldn't imagine how Jane must have felt living in it.

She pointed back to the bench. 'I was up there, leaving some flowers. Then I walked to the edge of the cliffs and screamed at the sea. I miss him so much.' She laughed. 'Then, when I came down the path, I bump into you, having a wee.'

'Yeah, again, sorry about that.'

Jane pulled out her phone. 'I hope this doesn't sound weird, but can I have your details? I don't know why. You might be a good person to talk to sometime. Or I can follow you on Instagram . . .'

'Of course.'

Jane smiled and assured me that she was OK. We hugged again and as I walked off, towards Joe's bench, a light rain shower broke apart in the morning sun and I took a moment to think about some of the mates I'd lost, blokes gone too soon – some of them in warfare, others through accidents, one or two because of their mental health. In my first post in the Marines, it was my role to help bring the coffins from the Hercules planes after they'd landed at RAF Brize Norton. The bodies inside were Marines returning from Iraq and the sight of those wooden boxes, draped in the Union Jack flag, was always a sobering reminder of war's impact. The funerals were traumatic. I must had done around 15 of them and the screams of the mothers as they watched their sons being lowered into the ground pierced my lungs and guts and yanked at my heart.

During one ceremony, a dead soldier of considerable size couldn't be laid to rest because the diggers hadn't prepared the grave properly. It was too small and the coffin became wedged as it was being lowered into the hole.

You had one fucking job, I thought, fuming at the incompetence and feeling for the traumatised family gathered on the sidelines.

These were blokes I hadn't known but I was shaken by the sight of every one.

Of the people I'd served with, one death sticks out. A guy who I'll call Danny here. A quiet, shy lad on the base at Faslane – where we were in place to protect the nuclear subs positioned there – he was often bullied by some of the older, more experienced Marines. This was the early 2000s, a different era, and there were one or two toxic characters in the squadron. To pass the time, all sorts of games were introduced, all of them designed to humiliate and terrify the unwilling participants. For example, a Marine caught leaving his cup behind, anywhere, would find themselves in trouble. The mug was placed on the top of the mess hall telly and the victim had to roll the dice to determine how many times he was to be 'reefed' – a punishment whereby his trousers were pulled down and his arse cheeks thrashed with a flip-flop. Having been the victim of one or two reefings in my military career, I can confirm they were very painful and bloody humiliating.

In another ritual, lads were forced to strip naked, apart from a gas mask. They then had to run around while a room full of testosterone-loaded men hurled eggs at them. Danny copped more than his unfair share of the abuse. He was quiet, shy and not long out of basic training. Even though he knew his stuff, he found it hard to survive in such a toxic environment and retreated into his shell. On some days he wouldn't talk to anyone. That gave the bullies even more reason to pick on him.

At the time I was manning the front desk on sentry, which was a bit like being an office clerk. The room where the 'desk' was stationed looked like a hotel lobby, except one drawer contained the keys to the armoury, which I had to guard at all costs. We were in a constant state of high alert due to Russian nuclear sub activity in the region and practice drills were arranged, often without us being alerted in advance. Once the sirens kicked off, it was the job of whoever was manning the desk to open the armoury. The squadron would then charge in and grab their weapons.

One morning, as I settled into another shift, the alarms sounded. The sound of stampeding boots echoed around the base and I opened the drawer for the armoury keys.

Shit. They weren't there.

I searched for them frantically, looking in drawers, under the paperwork and on the floor. When I walked nervously towards the armoury door, it was slightly ajar. The keys were dangling from the lock.

This can't be good, I thought, peering inside.

When I checked the racks, all the SA80s – the weapon of choice for the British military at the time – were in place. But when I turned the corner, I saw something that turned my stomach upside down. Danny was lying on his side, a lake of blood pooling around him. The poor guy had blown his brains out. God knows how long he'd been there. And when his possessions were cleared out and his diary was discovered, it turned out that he'd been broken by the bullying on the base. Danny couldn't handle it, and the senseless loss made me feel sick. I couldn't imagine the pain experienced by his parents.

Jane's circumstances were very different but the hurt she was enduring would have been just as acute. No parent should have to bury their child. But these tragedies couldn't be swept away. Jane had wanted to talk about Joe, and for good reason too. He sounded like a great guy, the sort of Marine I'd have enjoyed serving with, and I hoped that our conversation had helped her in some way, maybe even allowed her to enjoy Joe's life again. In other cultures and religions, such as Buddhism, or in Mexico, where they celebrate the Day of the Dead, the end isn't to be feared but celebrated, and conversations take place about it all the time.

I walked on with a new purpose in my heart. Joe was gone. My friends in the Marines were gone too. But by thinking and talking about them, I could keep them alive.

I just needed to seize the day and walk.

CHAPTER NINETEEN

A LITTLE HELP

I was on the stomp, ahead of schedule and walking hard across the border, where the weather pivoted sharply away from the long, hot summer days I'd enjoyed on the east coast of England into a week of ferocious rainstorms. I zipped up my windproof jacket and walked through each one, trying my best to stay positive, which was difficult in such treacherous conditions. I'd realised that familiarity had created a little contempt and retreading old ground was causing boredom to creep in. The voices whispered conspiratorially whenever the cold and wet became too much. 'You've done this all before,' they said. 'It's old hat. Just go home, no one's going to care.'

My heart sank on their arrival. *Oh man, this already?* I thought. *I can't be burned out yet. I'm not even into winter.*

I looked inwards to push the negativity away, resetting my attitude by listing the charities that were benefiting from my efforts. Then I thought of Jane and her son, Joe. 'This time,

I'm doing it for *them*,' I said. Finally, I reminded myself of the Scottish winter from the first loop and how its brutal temperatures had numbed my bones and muscles. Moving quickly through the autumn would save me from the West Highland Way and the NC500 at its most inhospitable, where I would be perilously alone and dangerously distanced from help. (Because very few people are mad enough to walk it during January and February.) If I took a wrong turn or injured myself, hypothermia and frostbite would become very real and very deadly concerns. That thought alone was enough to put a rocket up my arse. As was the buzz I received every time I told a stranger about my journey. *I am walking Britain – twice.* That always blew people's minds.

During my lowest moments, I turned to Instagram for moral support. At that stage in the walk, I had very little to prove to either myself or anyone else, and so reaching out for encouragement was hardly a dent to my ego. I had no problem admitting to my fears and uncertainties on social media when I was on a downer, especially when it was causing me to reflect and adjust. Chatting to Jane had caused some unpleasant memories to resurface. Remembering those coffins at Brize Norton had resulted in a painful flashback and thinking of Danny was reopening some old wounds too. I knew what could happen to a person when they suffered in silence – it was a dangerous hole I'd fallen into at the very start of The Path. I really didn't want to return.

I expressed my doubts and concerns through a series of vulnerable Instagram reels and posts that described some of the emotional obstacles I'd confronted. The work was cathartic and therapeutic, and I realised that by articulating my feelings, I could see them for what they truly were – symptoms of fatigue and loneliness. These were my psychological tripwires and stepping into them often resulted in a mental low. But help was at hand and the reaction to my public honesty was a series of empathetic, encouraging and supportive messages, some of them from people I'd already met, others from people I'd only spoken to online, while a handful arrived from people who had only just followed me. Instagram had become a pocket counsellor, sounding board and cheerleader rolled into one, and I used it to steady my mind during moments of turbulence. With every DM, I stepped further away from the shadows, knowing that while I was undoubtedly alone on The Path, I wasn't lonely.

In many ways, these emotions were completely understandable. I had already completed a life-changing lap of Great Britain, so it was only natural that the Victory Lap would feel weird, maybe even underwhelming. A level of emotional fatigue was my brain's natural response as the novelty of my challenge dissipated. Being a football fan, I knew all about the all-conquering sides, like United and their famous treble from 1999 (when they'd won the league, FA Cup and Champions League), and Manchester City in 2023. Despite exhausting themselves to go beyond all expectations, both sides had regrouped the following season and, in doing so, overcame the fatigue and found a way to win the Premier League once more. The hunger had been there. I would need to do the same and that clichéd phrase about 'digging deep' suddenly became incredibly appropriate.

At other times, an unexpected helping hand reached out from the Real World. One morning, as I strode away from the long grass somewhere on the trail to Edinburgh, zipping up my flies after yet another coffee-fuelled toilet break, my phone buzzed. I looked at the screen. The name 'Louis' flashed on the front. Though I wasn't sure at first, I suspected it was the Louis I'd met several weeks earlier while walking across the beach at Lowestoft. Back then, he'd started out as a shape in my peripheral vision, a figure moving at speed, dressed in shorts and t-shirt, half walking, half jogging. For a moment, I'd wondered if he was a mugger. Then he'd shouted out: 'Alright, Warrior?'

When I'd turned, the bloke was waving awkwardly. I stopped and waited for him to catch up.

'Hello, mate.'

'I'm Louis,' he'd said, shaking my hand. 'You met my mate Joey on the last day of your walk earlier in the year. Lymington. April?'

He'd been talking about one of the Three Amigos who had assisted me as I'd deliriously attempted to cross the finish line on that exhausting evening. 'Bloody hell!' I shouted. 'What the fuck are you doing here?'

Louis had laughed. 'I'm a soldier based down south but I live here. I've been following you ever since Joey mentioned it. What you're doing is awesome. Can I join you for a bit?'

I'd had no problem with that. The company was much appreciated.

Later that day, when I'd needed to rush ahead to a spot somewhere up the trail to collect the key for my next sleeping quarters (because the host had somewhere else to be), Louis had told me to relax. He then drove ahead and retrieved it for me. On a day when I'd been running on fumes following a 40km walk, his gesture had been a lifesaver. Louis was a stand-up bloke.

After our encounter, I wasn't sure if I would see him again. Some people on The Path came and went at the right time, and I never heard from them after that. Others stuck around and became good friends. Louis seemed to be in the latter group.

I stared at my phone. *Bloody hell*, I thought. *Why is he calling now?*

I pressed the 'ACCEPT' icon. 'Bro, how's it going?'

The coastal winds made it hard to hear anything on the other end. Then Louis' laughter cut through the noise. 'Mate, are you going to turn around or what?' he shouted.

I spun. There in the near distance was Louis. He was yomping towards me, waving, as was Joey, plus another bloke I didn't recognise. All three were wearing hiking kit and rucksacks. They looked like a crew of serious trekkers – muscular, lean, moving at speed. Instantly, a surge of appreciation flooded my body and my heart felt full for two people I barely knew. (But who had shown up for me in tough times.) I was also bloody confused. Louis and Joey lived miles away, and I had no clue who the other bloke was.

We hugged on The Path. 'I don't get it,' I said. 'What's this?'

Louis, breathing heavily, swigged on a bottle of water. He must have been walking at a serious pace. 'Well, I saw that message on Instagram a few days ago. I could tell you were struggling, feeling a bit demotivated. So, I called *him*.' Louis pointed to Joey.

Joey then pointed to the third man. 'And then *I* called *him*. This is Ant.'

'Which was when we decided, fuck it, he needs some help,' said Louis. 'We can't let you quit, bro.'

Joey explained how the three of them were mates from the army and followers of my Instagram account. They'd assessed my positional data, which included some stats from the website, the occasional map dropped onto Instagram, and a series of photos and pinned locations. Having taken an educated guess on where I might be, Joey set off from Portsmouth (where his military base was located) and collected Louis in Lowestoft and Ant in Leeds. They'd then driven overnight, all the way to somewhere close to Edinburgh, where, after spending much of the morning walking, I'd appeared ahead of them on the trail, moving at speed. Luckily, their military training had built the stamina to catch up.

I was stunned. *Bloody hell,* I thought. *What an effort.*

'We couldn't let you down,' said Louis. 'We wanted to give you a boost.'

Joey gave me a friendly shove. 'So, can we join you? See how far we get?'

'Course, mate!'

We walked and talked all day, drinking coffee and spinning stories until mid-afternoon. Joey, Louis and Ant eventually had to turn back for their parked car, so we said our farewells at a nearby station. But it wasn't a goodbye.

'Oi, Warrior. I've walked with you in England,' said Louis, 'We've walked with you in Scotland. Keep an eye out for us in Wales because we'll find you there too.'

I had zero doubts they would. 'This is the Brotherhood in action,' I said, referring to a term used by a lot of ex-Marines and soldiers to describe the link that bonded all of us. 'You knew I was struggling and you came out here to see me. Not everyone makes that effort. This was next level.'

Louis tried to shrug it off. 'It's what we do,' he said.

'Yeah. Maybe. But I've not heard from any of my family. You're strangers really – compared to them, anyway. You could have sent a message and that would have been enough. But coming up here, not telling me . . . It's given me a massive boost.'

We all hugged.

'You guys are proper mates,' I said, wishing I could walk with them forever.

* * *

These incredible gestures, big and small, usually appeared when they were most needed. As I made a charge for Edinburgh, I visited some of the people I'd stayed with during the first lap. In Musselburgh, I reunited with Anthony and his furry friend. I crashed in hotels gifted to me by strangers. I crashed in guest houses where the checkout bill came to zero. And I crashed on the sofas of old mates. As the early August weather careered between holiday heatwave and hibernation cold, my plan was still to get to John O'Groats, and my winter kit, as quickly as possible. A large chunk of the country had already been completed and while there was every chance I could escape Scotland before the dangerous weather really took hold, it was going to be tight. Reassuringly, I had a chance, thanks to the people, mates and strangers along The Path.

Sometimes, the little gestures turned out to be the most impactful of all. Despite my belief that I was refuelling like an athlete, I sometimes still made the odd schoolboy error. On some days, I burned through my food too quickly and struggled to maintain the pace, my stomach groaning and straining with hunger as low blood sugar brought on waves of fatigue. On others, I drained my water supply ahead of time and became dehydrated, which was problematic when I was miles away from the nearest town or beach hut.

On one occasion, shortly after leaving Edinburgh, I entered an area that felt like a food desert. The trail was deserted, the promenades were empty, even though we were in the thick of the school summer holidays, and as the afternoon turned hot, I realised I'd been walking for hours without passing a store or café. I was gasping and out of water. I felt my muscles creaking. A sweet shop appeared on the horizon but when I arrived – my mind imagining the sensation of a chilled bottle of water sloshing in my tummy (followed by an ice lolly and maybe a second ice lolly) – the place was shut. By the looks of things, it had been out of business for months.

I pushed on, eventually passing a bungalow cut into the clifftop. In the front garden, sitting on his bench, was an elderly bloke dressed in shorts and a button-down shirt. His summery vibe was completed by a pair of sunglasses and cap. With his garden hose in one hand and a cuppa in the other, he looked like the most relaxed man on the planet. By contrast, I was at the end of a 45km day, feeling nauseous in the heat and dangerously thirsty. My t-shirt was soaked through. My tongue felt like a strip of sandpaper.

'I'm so sorry to disturb you,' I croaked, in my politest voice.

The man turned off his hose and came to the edge of the garden boundaries. A small, neatly trimmed hedge divided us. 'Yes, laddie?'

'Um, any chance I could get a glass of water?' I pointed back down the track. 'I wanted to stock up at the shop down there, but it was closed.'

The man smiled kindly. 'Of course,' he said. 'You're lucky I'm gardening, there's nothing around here for miles.'

Having returned with a full pint glass, he watched in surprise as I downed the lot in one go. 'Hmm, better get you another,' he said, walking back to the kitchen, laughing as he did so.

We must have repeated the process three more times until my thirst was fixed. If I hadn't been soaked through with sweat, I'd have hugged him tightly.

CHAPTER TWENTY

ALICE

Dundee ticked all the boxes for me.

Historical architecture, check.

Cool coffee shops, check.

Funky museums, art, good food, check, check, check.

I spent a day or two walking about the city, hanging out until the moon had come up. As much as I loved the mornings, with their dappling light shows and an overwhelming sense of optimism – twinned with that buzzy caffeine rush – I also enjoyed the sun's last gasps, especially as the shadows lengthened and the sky turned into a bonfire of reds, oranges and purples. I'd nicknamed this moment the Witching Hour because magic tended to happen within it: people reached out with weird suggestions, The Path's more interesting characteristics revealed themselves, and life became transformative and spectral.

It was during this time, while wandering through Dundee,

that an exciting message appeared on Instagram. One that would change my life forever:

@Alice: *Hey Warrior Walker!*

I've discovered your profile. I love what you're about. I love what you're doing. You've chosen the lonely path, but I get it, it's the best way.

Keep doing what you're doing. When you get to Bristol, I'd love to go for a beer or a coffee with you.

Alice

Instagram: 19 August 2023

Wow, I thought. *What a nice thing to say.*

In a knee-jerk reaction, I checked Alice's profile page and scrolled through one or two pictures while reading the captions. *Bloody hell, she was cute!* Alice had a beautiful smile and sparkly eyes, long dark hair and piercings. Her look was on the arty side; she might even have been a bit hippy-ish. Another picture revealed Alice to be a tattoo artist working in Bristol, which seemed like a cool job. In every image she was surrounded by friendly-looking people, a reliable indicator of an all-round good person. I picked up on a nice energy immediately and my body was soon awash with happy chemicals. I loved all of it. And that was . . . *weird.* I tried to think of a time when I'd last felt this excited but couldn't remember one.

Just as I was about to write back a thank you, hoping to find out a little more, my phone buzzed.

It was Alice. Again.

@**Alice:** *By the way, this isn't one of <u>those</u> thirsty messages. I'm not flirting. I'm just interested in what you're doing.*
Alice
Instagram: 19 August 2023

I sighed and pocketed the phone. *My response can wait, then.* The fact that Alice hadn't wanted to come across as being 'thirsty' was a sign that her intentions were supportive and nothing more. Those butterflies in my stomach were probably a false signal. And the fact that she was cool, friendly and bloody cute was something I could probably get over quite quickly if I put my mind to it. Also, the last thing I wanted was to send a flirtatious message back, become caught up in an online tangle – that's if someone as hot as Alice would even consider a bloke like me – and distract myself from the primary mission. The Path was my priority and winter was coming. Plus, I'd learned my lesson from the first lap, when mixed signals and crossed wires had put me in one or two embarrassing situations.

So why do I feel disappointed?

I scrabbled around in my jacket for the phone again. There was something about Alice that made me want to respond, like, *immediately.* Convincing myself that I was only really interested in getting another tattoo, maybe a commemorative motif of The Path, I texted back:

@**thewarriorwalker:** *Thanks! I'd love to get a tattoo . . .*
Paul
Instagram: 19 August 2023
Short, sweet, simple. *Why say anything else?*

For the next few days, there were no messages from Alice and, as expected, I did a pretty good job of sidestepping the fact that she was cool, friendly, and bloody cute. My objective was to walk The Path in a year and no person, place or perspective was going to get in the way. For a day or two, my resolve remained untested. Then Alice messaged again and that resolve crumbled. We had one or two chats during the first week, before upping the frequency to one or two messages a day, and then one or two an hour. I wasn't sure what was happening but every contact felt like a little charge of electricity. I tingled with excitement for hours afterwards. I also became twitchy with anxiety because I really didn't want to become sidetracked.

Something about Alice was sticking with me, though. *I think I fancy her,* I thought. I found myself looking at her photos and wondering who she really was. I couldn't get her out of my head, even though we hadn't physically met. She was a tractor beam; I felt magnetised.

By the time August had faded away, I was yomping towards Inverness, where Paul was waiting to drive me to Stoer. Once again, my plan was to use his cottage as a base camp while walking the NC500, this time in reverse order, moving from Inverness up to John O'Groats, then along Scotland's northern edge before arcing down to Ullapool. From there my plan was to return to Lewis and Harris, and Skye before completing the rest of Scotland, via the West Highland Way and Glasgow, then passing through Kilmarnock and Dumfries before crossing the border. I'd last seen Paul, face to face, in February, and when we met in an Inverness café, the pair of us hugged, drank coffee and talked through the highlights of the past six months. It was so good to see him, and we had plenty to chat about. And once I'd detailed my itinerary for the coming months, he had one or two probing questions.

'So . . . any interesting friends. *Girls?*' he said. 'You must get a lot of attention now?'

Without even thinking, I responded: 'Yeah, there's one. She's called Alice . . .'

My answer was a shock. *Where the hell had that come from?* We'd only messaged via social media. It wasn't as if we'd even met. And yet, as I told Paul everything I knew about Alice, it was in a way that suggested something much more significant was taking place. Maybe it was wishful thinking, maybe it was excitement, maybe I somehow knew our meeting was inevitable and authored by the universe. I'm not entirely sure. Paul, thankfully, didn't press for any more details. The revelation was swept aside, suspended in midair, leaving me to analyse the ins and outs of those texts and chats with Alice. *Is my subconscious giving me a clue?* The truth was uncertain but something in my immediate orbit was undoubtedly shifting.

Meanwhile, our Instagram chats were becoming increasingly vulnerable. Alice revealed how she'd first noticed me when a mate had shared one of my reels online. I'd been explaining my hopes for the Victory Lap at the time and after hearing me talk, she'd scrolled through my posts. This made me feel less weird about having scrolled through hers. Alice later explained how she'd wanted to get in touch but wasn't entirely sure why. I knew that feeling. Both of us were clearly wanderers, the type of people who moved into communities and relationships and then moved out of them again. With these details, our connection intensified.

The Instagram messages moved onto WhatsApp, then voice notes, but not phone calls – at least, not yet. As I walked further around the NC500 and autumn became a fact rather than a rumour, I felt as if something special was building. But I had no idea of its potential or direction.

Because I've not met her.

Maybe it was Alice, or maybe it was because I was beginning to wonder what might happen after the Victory Lap, but I began looking too far ahead, to some unspecified point in the future, when I'd found a house, a permanent position on the map and a community of my own.

Where do you want to live?

What sort of person do you want to be?

What type of person do you want to share your life with?

Mostly, the answers were hardly surprising. Part of me wanted to live in the southwest. I thought about setting up base with Nicola and David as I looked around North Devon for a job and a rental flat. Then I imagined living somewhere near to Alice in Bristol and my body jolted in surprise. *Well, this is new,* I thought. Wanting to figure out my thought process, I called her straight away, something I hadn't yet done. (Though she had made it clear I could.) I wanted to hear her voice; I needed to tell her my thoughts and feelings. Luckily for me, Alice didn't freak out and she agreed that something was happening. But in a way, that weirded me out even more.

Because I've not met her.

I was spinning. My stomach tickled nervily with butterflies

over an intangible link with someone I hadn't even hugged, let alone kissed. And it was romantic – *right?* It was definitely unusual, and unexpected, and nice. So, I told her. Exactly that. In those words. And the chat lasted for hours, all of it beautiful, terrifying and weird.

Because I've not met her.

Was I overreaching? It was hard not to feel as if I might be imagining things that weren't there. I wondered if exhaustion was contributing to my emotional state. There was also the possibility that my time outdoors, wandering alone in the wilderness, had sent me a little doolally. But, as far as I was concerned, the relationship between Alice and me had leapt over the initially awkward but euphoric phase (we could get *there* later) and into a stage where early plans were being made. That night, we talked about the friends we'd like to introduce to one another. Interesting locations were suggested for our first, second and third dates. (Because we were definitely going on at least one.) At one point, we even drew up a list of dream holiday destinations, like a serious couple. Part of me worried that I was giving too much of myself away, especially after my painful break-up with Joy. I really didn't want to get hurt again, but I also believed that the big decisions in life should be based on opportunity rather than fear. Alice felt like a big decision. I wanted to explore every possibility, rather than retreating from my emotions.

When I woke up at 11am, the morning after our epic call, feeling exhausted, the first thing I did was to reread the messages I'd received from Alice over the past few weeks. 'I hope last night's chat wasn't a dream?' I typed.

Alice wrote back immediately: 'No, it wasn't.'

Three dots appeared. Alice was typing. My heart thumped.

'So, I guess we'll have to do it all again tonight?' she said.

* * *

As I continued around the north coast of Scotland, Alice was dialled into every small victory. I messaged her when I reached John O'Groats and its symbolic signpost. Whenever I spotted a stag, I sent emojis and pics. She was as much a part of The Path as the sound of the sea and the roaring winds. Clearly, chatting to Alice hadn't altered my focus whatsoever. I was now weeks ahead of schedule and set to clear the most northerly parts of Scotland and the West Highland Way before the season's most gruesome weather arrived. But this aggressive pace came with an expensive price tag. I was edging closer to burnout and spending time with Paul reminded me of those grim weeks when my knee had buckled and the muscles and ligaments had snagged and pinched painfully. The time to take a break was approaching.

Then one evening, Alice texted with a surprising note: 'Hey. I'm going to fly up to Scotland on Sunday. I want to see you.'

My heart stopped. Of all the things I'd expected to happen that day (a long walk, aching feet, a growling stomach, dehydration, followed by a long sleep), Alice's announcement hadn't been on the list. And yet, I didn't hesitate. The time to push things forward had arrived. To do anything else would have killed our momentum.

'OK, do it.'

The three dots appeared again. 'Great! I need to know if this is real.'

Suddenly, the butterflies in my stomach grew into a flock of small birds. I realised that this was a storyline from a

Hollywood film, rather than something that happened in real life. I was excited, no doubt, but anxious. Happy, but nervous. Optimistic, but stressed at the thought of doing something that might screw everything up. So, I did everything I could to calm myself down. I assured myself that I was safe: Alice knew that I'd been in a weird headspace for a long period of time and that I'd come close to ending it all. She also understood that I was on a journey of healing but not yet healed. Though hearing about my backstory on the phone was an altogether different experience to seeing it up close. *Would she like me?* I reminded myself that I was a very different person to the one who had experienced a panic attack in Glasgow two years previously. I was stronger. I walked taller. I held conversations and looked people in the eye. Alice liked me for who I was. I decided to be that person when meeting her for real.

The following morning, as Paul made coffee and readied our snacks for yet another day serving as captain of the Warrior Walker Support Wagon, I blurted out the latest development.

'We've got to drive to Inverness at the weekend,' I said.

He put down his mug and leaned against the kitchen work-top. 'Oh, OK. And why's that?'

A huge grin spread across my face. 'Alice is coming up to see me.'

Paul ran over for a hug. 'That's fantastic, mate! I'm so pleased for you. Well, that's quite a leap. . .'

'I know . . . I think we just decided to see if it was real or a bit of a fantasy. So, it could be great, but it could be weird.'

Paul looked at me seriously. Something important was coming. 'Given all of that . . .'

'Yeah? Go on . . .'

'Where is she sleeping?'

I froze. Working out the bed arrangements hadn't even come into my mind. In all our conversations, the delicate matter of who would sleep where wasn't discussed once. I didn't want to seem presumptuous but I didn't want to come across as indifferent, or standoffish either. In the early stages of previous relationships, I'd sometimes felt weird about sleeping in the same bed as someone I really liked, which was very much the case with Alice. I suddenly stressed that I might fidget, or talk in my sleep, or fart at the worst possible moment. At that time, I also felt guarded and protective of my own space, which was probably another symptomatic response to the meltdown I'd experienced in 2020, as well as the fact that I'd spent so much time travelling solo on The Path. While working with Simon at his Portscatho Beach restaurant, I'd had a brief relationship with someone in the area. Whenever it came to bedtime, I couldn't relax. A lot of the time, I slept on the sofa because it was far less stressful.

Paul noticed my discomfort. 'Don't worry about it, I'll put her in one of the cottages for now,' he said. 'We're quiet and there are no guests this weekend. You can figure it out afterwards.'

He went to his office, opened the laptop and marked the cottage as being booked. What he didn't tell me was that he couldn't remember Alice's surname from our previous conversations. Several months later, he revealed his unusual entry for her in the guest register, laughing as he did so.

Welcome to Stoer, Mrs Alice Harris.

CHAPTER TWENTY-ONE

BOOK CLUB

The late October rain slapped and plopped against the car roof. The wipers squeaked, the heater whooshed and my stomach flip-flopped noisily. I was sitting in the passenger seat of Paul's car, the pair of us waiting in the dark by a café in Inverness town centre, waiting for Alice to arrive. I was knackered, having spent several days walking on the NC500 in the pouring rain. More exhausting was my mental state, as I switched from intense excitement to abject terror at the thought of Alice transforming from a disembodied voice on the phone into a living, breathing, three-dimensional person.

Paul turned in his seat. 'Any thoughts, mate?'

'Yeah,' I said, staring at the streetlights in the distance. 'I'm absolutely shitting myself.' I felt close to panicking. 'What if she doesn't like me?'

He laughed. 'Well, we've already established that's not the case, seeing as you've been speaking for a couple of months.'

'Yeah, but what if she doesn't like me as much as I like her? Or what if I don't like her at all?' I groaned loudly. 'I think I'm going to throw up . . .'

Paul put his arm on my shoulder. He was laughing. 'How do you feel about the walk now? Like, have the past few weeks changed anything for you? Any lessons?'

'Thanks, but no,' I said, cutting him off. 'I know what you're doing.'

Paul was trying his best to look innocent. It wasn't working. '*What?* I'm interested.'

'Yeah. But you're also trying to focus me on something other than—'

'Shit.' Paul had bolted upright in his seat. '*Shit.*'

'What? *What?*'

'She's here, mate.' He turned to face me. 'She's bloody here!' But I was already halfway out of the car. Alice was running towards me – a living, breathing, actual person. She jumped on me, wrapped her arms around my neck and kissed me on the cheek. And all those doubts about whether she'd like me or if I'd like her had washed away in the rain.

* * *

Alice had flown to Inverness from Bristol and picked up a hire car. As we drove towards Stoer, Paul leading the way in the wet, the talk was non-stop. I think we only paused to admire a stag by the roadside, its eyes reflecting in our headlights like laser beams.

'*See?* I wasn't kidding,' I said, pointing. 'There's loads of them up here.'

Whenever I looked across at Alice in the green glow of her dashboard lights, my chest felt heavy. For a moment I was lightheaded, almost dizzy. *Am I dreaming?* I thought. I knew I couldn't wait to see her in the light. And when I did, in the headlights of a passing car, she looked beautiful, all those Instagram pictures, the best bits, coming to life up close. Bright colours. Sharp edges. With sights and smells and light touches. I felt overwhelmed at the emotional leap and questioned every word that came out of my mouth because I already felt as if I liked her too much. *What the actual hell?* I thought. *How is this going to work?* Whether Alice was thinking the same thing I really couldn't tell, but there was a connection between us. I could feel it sparking. And after dinner, when I walked her to the Airbnb croft, she invited me inside.

Oh my god, I thought. *Are we going to sleep together?*

I could feel the energy between us, which was amazing because I really fancied her, and I was desperate to make everything special and memorable. But I became so nervous, so smothered by the intensity of the moment that my body, *the most important part,* failed to work at the worst possible moment.

Alice squeezed my hand as we hugged on the bed afterwards. 'Don't worry about it,' she said. 'It's fine. Give me a hug.'

I felt terrible. Being so in my head had short-circuited my sex drive at the worst possible time and I went into a spiral.

Alice squeezed me even tighter. 'Hey, it's OK,' she said. When I looked up at her, she was smiling. 'It's not surprising this has happened.'

'Are you sure? Because I feel terrible. Like, really embarrassed.'

Alice shook her head. 'Don't. *This*. It's a lot. But being here with you is *enough*.'

We stayed there for hours, until I went to my room and slept in my own bed, alone, with all my anxieties for company. Then I messaged Alice to make sure everything was OK.

'This is amazing,' I said. 'I don't want it to end.'

My phone pinged instantly. 'Me neither.'

* * *

When I woke up the next morning, Alice had risen early. She'd started her day by going for a walk. I had zero doubts that she was the person for me.

Talking, talking, talking. It's all we did on that first day – and it felt amazing. There were no awkward silences, no jarring comments, no *what the hell?* opinions. Alice was so sharply dialled into my unusual frequencies that it felt unusual, and I felt confused and off balance. *Why is this happening now?* It almost seemed as if the universe was testing me. It wanted to know whether I possessed the commitment to stick to The Path, with all its solitude, hard miles and ferocious storms, by placing a beautiful human in the way. I suddenly had an affinity with the fictional sailors I'd once read about in children's books, determined, strong-willed blokes lured to their death on the rocks by mermaids singing to them from the shallows. I felt more at home with Alice than with anyone – or anywhere.

I learned so much about her in those first 24 hours. I loved the way she kissed me. She had a free and creative spirit that made me want to be free and creative too. Her smile radiated kindness and she talked with her eyes. They were a deep hazel. She had travelled the world and visited places as far away as New Zealand, Cambodia and Costa Rica. Every word brimmed with hope and optimism and enthusiasm. She enjoyed swimming in the sea, walking in nature and scruffling dogs as they passed us on the trail. Alice even loved her morning coffee. Sometimes it was as if we'd been forced together by fate because, *come on,* how could two random strangers be any more suited to one another?

The temptation to drop my bag for Alice and to travel to Bristol for good was creeping into my thoughts because she understood me so deeply. When I freaked out about how naturally everything was falling into place, she nodded her head and smiled because she was freaking out too. When I admitted to worrying that everything was maybe moving too fast, she admitted to feeling the same way. When I told her that this was day one of our story, and that every story had to start somewhere, she knew exactly what I was talking about. Alice even sensed my discomfort at what had happened in bed the night before. My male ego had been bruised. No bloke wants to experience an attack of pre-match nerves, especially not on a first date. That only happened to old dudes in Viagra commercials. Every now and then, my cringe caused me to overthink and self-analyse, but whenever I became broody, Alice grabbed my hand or cuddled me.

'You're thinking about last night, aren't you?' she said.

Yeah. 'Maybe,' I lied. 'A little bit.'

'Well don't. You'd be surprised how often it happens to people.'

She was right. But most men won't admit it. Or they struggle to discuss the event fully with their partner because their pride has taken charge. However, I knew it was important to shake off the shame and negative feelings because they would only grow and fester otherwise. In such a situation, the issue of my erection, or lack of, would become overly stressful and I'd find myself trapped in a flywheel of doom. When a person becomes so worried about whether their body is going to work, it inevitably fails them at the worst possible moment.

As I showed Alice my favourite places around Stoer, like the beach and the old burial grounds, I couldn't stop thinking about how much I fancied her. I really didn't want to screw it up. Later that night, as we relaxed in her room, kissing and cuddling, she pulled a book from the nearby shelf.

'Why don't we do a book club?' she said.

'Er, sure. What does that involve, exactly?'

Alice smiled. I must have looked uncertain about where this was leading. 'Well, I pick a book and read it for a bit. You pick a book and read it for a bit. And then we'll talk about the books we're reading. What we like. What we don't like. That sort of thing.'

Sounds good, I thought. I'd always been a big reader. I walked over to one of Paul's bookshelves and scanned the colourful spines for something of interest, hoping to find a Cold War spy thriller or some spiritual narrative that encouraged the reader to see the world in a different light. It was quite a range. Luckily, he had a library for all tastes, a nice touch in any Airbnb. I reached out and pulled down a book. Alice grabbed another. Both of us sat on the edge of the bed and managed a few lines each – but the reading didn't last for long. With the distraction of the book club, everything started moving exactly as it was supposed to, and when we collapsed in a tangle under the covers, I couldn't stop smiling.

'What?' laughed Alice.

But she knew exactly what.

'It works!' I said, doing my best not to shout. 'It bloody works!'

She held me tighter than ever before.

* * *

One evening turned into five as the term 'Book Club' became a codeword for intimacy, though we still slept in separate beds because my anxieties hadn't settled. And yet everything felt so exciting. I didn't want Alice to leave and when the time arrived, I suggested maybe going with her. I wanted to see what her life in Bristol looked like.

'You can't do that,' she said firmly. 'You need to finish the walk.'

'I can,' I said. 'Because I've got to take some more rest. It doesn't matter if I relax here in Scotland or if I come to Bristol to see you.'

But Alice stayed firm. 'No. I know where this is going and you're not breaking off your walk because of me. Stick to the plan.'

'Yeah, but I take breaks from time to time,' I said. 'Christmases at Nicola and David's, here. I can—'

But Alice was still shaking her head. 'No, Paul. If you don't finish this, I'll feel terrible. The Path is important. And I really don't want a load of trolls blaming me on social media if you stop.'

She was right, I knew it, but I was scared to let her go. Equally, I'd have been scared to go with her because I was falling in love, and it wasn't easy for me to access those emotions. My past relationships had been fragmented. I'd found it tough to let someone fully into my life, especially while serving in the Marines when I'd spent long periods away from home. I'm ashamed to say I even cheated once or twice. But the single life was just as confusing. My break-up with Joy had left me feeling isolated, vulnerable and frightened. Meanwhile, Alice was a conundrum: both the best thing in the world because she was so beautiful, inside and out, and the worst because of my fears. When she left, I experienced an undeniable physical pain. It hurt to think of the empty, person-shaped hole alongside me, more than my aching back and swollen feet.

'I'll never get bored of you,' I texted shortly after her departure, as I walked the tail end of the NC500. 'I'll never not want to see you.'

I meant it, too.

The first lap of Britain had shown me, deep down, that 1) I loved people, and 2) I placed a high value on my alone time. Of the two, I'd previously believed that alone time was the most important thing. Alice was the first person to make me rethink that balance and I struggled to remember a time when I'd felt so entirely me. I was fully present in her company and at one with myself. I honestly couldn't wait to see her again. For now, though, we were on totally different trails. I had my transient life to explore, with Scotland and the western side of the British coastline still to go. That would be followed shortly afterwards by Wales, the South West Coast Path and the long slog towards London. Meanwhile, Alice had her life in Bristol at the tattoo studio. For now, our commitments had divided us.

As I trudged around the NC500, I had a hunch it wouldn't be for long.

CHAPTER TWENTY-TWO

WHAT'S MEANT FOR YOU WON'T PASS YOU BY

Alice had come to me from out of nowhere and suddenly she was everywhere. There were reminders of her all over the place – in my kit bag, on The Path, even the smell of her perfume on my clothes – when only a week previously she'd been an almost intangible, digital presence. *That's the problem with meeting people through social media*, I thought. *Most of the time, they don't meet up to an imagined reality. When they do, it's intoxicating.* In this case, Alice had more than lived up to the mental picture I'd created for her during our WhatsApp chats and phone calls. Now she was gone, a massive Alice-shaped void had appeared in my life.

And it bloody hurt.

All the old aches and injuries came back at once. My knee throbbed painfully. The muscles, ligaments and tendons in my legs twanged and grabbed, like I was clenching for impact with some unseen obstacle and my walking pace slowed. Emotionally, I felt upended too. A week earlier, I'd been moving along The Path at a rapid pace, delighted with my position in life, feeling in the flow and excited by the world around me. Suddenly, a beautiful other had arrived, a course correction I was desperate to make, and that same world was now complicated and full of new and unexpected challenges. The fears I'd previously expressed to Ann in Dale, almost two years ago to the day, now seemed foolish. There *was* a special someone in my future. The idea of having a family of my own suddenly *didn't* seem as unlikely as it once had. But there was no doubt Alice's appearance had created a list of questions about my long-term goals.

Among them was the sticky issue of where I might live after finishing The Path. Nicola and David in North Devon were the closest thing I had to a proper family. Moving near to them still felt like an option. I'd fallen in love with Scotland and, during my first walk of the NC500, I enjoyed a daydream where I met a local girl in some remote village and settled down near to Paul's place in Stoer. The pace of life there suited me, the people were amazing and Paul now felt more like a brother than a mate. But meeting Alice had changed my thinking and I was now considering Bristol, her hometown, as a suitable fit for someone like me. And if that was the case, where would I work? What would I do? And how would I find a new purpose? The logistics of home-hunting, household bills and job applications crashed into my life.

Then there was the nagging doubt that I might have been

making more of the situation than was rational, realistic or even healthy. I'd only known Alice for five minutes. *Am I getting carried away?* I thought. I immediately told my inner critic to pipe down. Allowing myself to be romantic and passionate was OK because that was the whole point of living. It also helped to remind myself of a saying that Nan had once shared with me as a kid: *What's meant for you won't pass you by.* I took it as a reminder that if Alice and I were being brought together by the universe, then everything was going work out regardless. That didn't help with the nervous churning in my stomach though, or the fluttery tightness in my chest. I missed her badly and wanted to hear her voice all the time.

This emotional turbulence soon became another learning curve. During my life's lowest moments, I'd often freaked out because so many of the things that were making me unhappy had been uncontrollable, like my forced departure from Thailand or the Covid lockdowns in 2020. Since then, I did everything to micromanage my circumstances in every aspect. Even the act of stepping outside my front door and yomping across the British coastline had been a way of claiming control. That same mindset tended to appear during my happiest moments too, and now I was no longer the sole master of my own destiny, anxiety crept in. There was another person involved, someone I cared for deeply, and relinquishing emotional control tweaked at my insecurities and restarted my imposter syndrome. I was frightened of losing a good thing.

Mentally, I was spiralling and rapidly approaching a breaking point, and everyone I spoke to could see it. Despite my recuperative week with Alice, I was physically wrecked, having got so far ahead of schedule by skipping the rest days I'd set aside for myself. In June, July and August I'd felt great. I was strong and highly motivated through September and October. But my body had been keeping the score and I was now paying a heavy price.

Every day I called Alice and explained my thoughts and emotions. Her responses only amplified the belief that I'd finally found a person suited to me, because she thought the exact same way. Eventually, I took the advice being dished out by my mates, old and new, and decided to take a holiday. Shortly after Alice had gone home in early November, I checked out the flight prices from Inverness to Bristol. I had to know if everything about her, and us, was real.

'I miss you every day,' I told her one morning, during another excitable phone call.

Alice sighed. 'I feel the same.'

Then I explained my plans to take some time off from The Path, to rest my body and mind, and to spend some more time with her.

'I'm looking at flights,' I said.

'Oh my god . . .'

'Yeah. I want to come down in a couple of days.'

Alice suddenly sounded concerned. 'But we talked about it. The walk. Your target. I don't want to stop you from doing this—'

I wasn't having it. Some things in life were more important. 'That's irrelevant. I'm so far ahead of where I'm supposed to be on the map that it makes sense to take a break. My body needs to recover. I'm just choosing to take my rest days with you in Bristol rather than somewhere else.'

I took a deep breath. 'And I'm curious to know more – about you, how you live, how *we* might live.'

'Like a dress rehearsal?' Alice sounded buzzy.

Exactly. 'You made the effort to come up here and lived my life for a week. Now I want to do the same for you and live your life. That way I can see if we fit in.'

There was a silence. I knew she was thinking things over. 'Just do it,' Alice said eventually.

I felt the happy chemicals charging through my body again. 'Yeah?'

She was laughing. 'Yeah!'

In a rush, I booked my flights and a few days later, I arrived in Bristol. I wanted to know whether it was a potentially happy place for me. Alice was at work, I had a few hours to kill, but as I sat in one of the airport's cafés, my intuition told me a worrying story. When I'd previously walked through the city during my first lap, I hadn't felt any sort of gravitational pull towards Bristol. I wasn't sure why. All I knew was that it didn't feel like the city for me. Thankfully, those early warning signs disappeared when I arrived at Alice's flat. The door key had been stashed under a flowerpot and I let myself in. Her place was cosy. There was so much of who she was to take in: Alice's own art was on display, there were other prints on the walls and her shelves were stuffed with books written by adventurous, explorer types. I saw a Levison Wood autobiography, another by Alastair Humphreys. *You can tell a lot about a person by the books they read,*

I thought. From what I was seeing, Alice and I were on the same page.

I dropped my bag, stuck my head in the bedroom and felt the familiar knot of anxiety in my gut. I looked back at the sofa in the living room and realised it wasn't big enough for a man of my height. Then I looked at the bed and its fresh sheets. *Oh god*, I thought. *I'm going to be sleeping in there.* Whether I liked it or not, I was spending the first night next to Alice, and to hell with the social embarrassment of fidgeting, snoring and farting. Not wanting to rummage around too much, I walked back into the kitchen and noticed a handwritten note pinned to the fridge door.

My Love
I hope your flight was good and smooth.
Welcome to Casa de Alicia. (I've never called it that before, but I like it – it's shocking.)
Make yourself at home and help yourself to anything. Mi casa es su casa. If you want a shower, there are clean towels in the right cupboard in the wardrobe. If you need a light on in the other room, it's the switch by the sofa. I haven't bought a bulb since March for the main light. LOL.
I love you.
See you soon.
Your Alice

The light outside had dimmed to a wintery dark blue. The streetlights were on. Then a bright white beam swept across the walls. Alice had pulled up in her car and my heart jackhammered. When she opened the door and kissed me, everything clicked into place. I smelled Alice's smells and felt her touches again. My body tingled with anticipation.

'What do you think of the place?' she said excitedly.

I told her I loved the books on her shelves. That her art was amazing. Then I overshared my anxieties about us sleeping in the same bed for the very first time because there was nowhere else for me to go.

'God, this is actually real now,' I said.

Alice hugged me. 'Just be yourself. It's fine. Don't worry about it.'

I felt reassured. The knot in my stomach relaxed.

When bedtime came, I jostled alongside her for a minute or two and then fell into a deep sleep, not waking until Alice had made coffee the next morning. I'd found safety. I'd found love. I was doing good.

* * *

I stayed with Alice for ten days, the pair of us exploring her world in Bristol. But whenever I checked the calendar and my progress across the map, I experienced a weird, doomy sensation. Despite an impressive headstart to the Victory Lap, my distances had dropped off in November, and I was now several days behind schedule. While my overall targets were still in play, the immediate challenges now facing me were immense. The autumn chill had turned to a winter freeze and there was a chance my time on the West Highland Way would be a horror show – all sub-zero temperatures and waist-high snow drifts. I'd previously collected some winter kit in John O'Groats, as planned, but it was piecemeal and unsuited to the grisly conditions. A few thermal tops, some waterproof outerwear and an insulated coat probably weren't going to be enough. Stroudy, my old mate from the Commandos Royal Marines Training Centre in Lympstone, would have gone spare at my lack of preparation.

Not wanting to dwell on the 'what ifs' too much, I headed back to Paul's and completed the final stretch of the NC500. I had a fire in my belly because there was now extra motivation for everything I was doing. Once my walk was complete, Alice and I had decided we were going to start a new life together. The yomp was still hard-going though: when I'd arrived on the island of Lewis and Harris, the sun barely seemed to rise above the horizon, the cold was biting and debilitating, and my skin goose-bumped and prickled in the icy winds. I used Alice as my inspiration on every incline and while walking up a vertiginous hill in the almost-dark, my back aching, the exposed flesh on my face burning, she rang with a suggestion. Would I like to join her at a work Christmas party next month?

'Oh my god, I'd love to,' I said. 'I'm nearly fucking dying out here.'

Plans were made. Once Christmas arrived in a few weeks, we'd travel back to Bristol to spend the holidays together and I could rejoin The Path afterwards. The trip sounded incredible. I would meet her friends and her family; we even made plans to visit her grandparents for Christmas dinner. Any doubts I'd had about the velocity of our relationship were now forgotten, though Alice was determined to pin me to my mission.

'I'm not going to see you again until we go back to Bristol for Christmas,' she said finally.

That felt like years away. 'Why? Surely we can arrange something?' I spluttered.

'Because you need to stick to the promise you made to yourself, to get this done in a year. It's time to focus.'

Her idea, while sensible, was a painful reality check and as I walked across Lewis and Harris, my life became a whole lot harder. The conditions were worsening, the heaviest of the weather had arrived slightly ahead of time and I was stepping into Scotland's remotest corners at their most fearsome. Prior to meeting Alice, the mantra I'd repeated to myself was that a harsh winter was coming and to avoid certain horrors, I'd have to move fast. In the bliss of connecting with such a beautiful human, that warning had been lost to the winds. And now I was screwed.

Winter had come.

CHAPTER TWENTY-THREE

HUMANS CAN DO HARD THINGS

After an amazing and restorative Christmas spent with Alice and her friends and family, I returned to The Path. Then the snow swept in. In Skye, where I stayed in a room provided by Andrew and Rich from The Coffee Bothy, I moved through a world of white. The island's mountains, lakes and undulating tracks sparkled and shimmered in the mists, and as I walked, my senses folded in on themselves. Every noise was muffled by a blanket of powdery drifts. At times, it was hard to see a way forward as I became snow blind. Unable to determine which way was up, I was forced to rely on my old-school route maps for guidance. In the plunging temperatures, my phone battery drained at a rapid rate and its GPS became unreliable as I moved in and out of reception. Thanking the stars for David's foresight, I unfolded his paper map and attempted to estimate my present location, the tips of my fingers numbing in the cold as they tracked the confusing paths and lines across the page. Everything I'd hoped to avoid – the freeze, the dark, the brutality of winter – was suddenly a very clear and present danger.

I walked north to south, while cursing my complacency – the risks were everywhere. Unable to see too far ahead, there was every chance I might stray from the track and become lost, or, worse, step into an unseen drop in the landscape and seriously injure myself or plunge to my end. Everything was doubly difficult. Keeping my feet dry was impossible; I might as well have been wading through shin-deep water. Staying warm was just as tricky; the weather app on my phone showed temperatures as low as -10C and I kicked myself for not performing a more thorough winter kit update when I'd had the chance. Yes, I had enough clothing to keep me alive but when it came to shelter, I was winging it at the worst possible time.

If I was forced to sleep rough at any point through some poor twist of fate, such as taking a wrong turn or not reaching a house or Airbnb in time (and, so far, I'd only been offered a room for my first night), I didn't even have a tent for shelter. To travel light, I'd also foregone a sleeping bag, a choice I now realised was potentially fatal, though my thinking had seemed logical at the time. To walk quickly, I needed a relatively light backpack. I genuinely believed it was possible to avoid the worst of the weather by moving at a rapid pace. My plan was now falling apart at the seams. But rather than hammering myself for it, I leaned into the belief that if anyone could overcome these conditions, it was me.

There were looks of concern everywhere I went. As I booted

it through the midpoint of Skye, a black Audi beeped its horn and pulled over ahead of me. The window wound down as I caught up and a smiling woman waved from across the passenger seat.

'Hello, Warrior Walker,' she shouted over the blast of her radio. 'Sorry, you don't know me. I'm Zoe.'

I stared at her blankly, feeling disorientated. 'Hi, Zoe.'

'I've been following you on Instagram for a bit and I saw you were walking Skye.'

I thought back to the reel I'd posted earlier that day. Zoe must have worked out my location from there. Now she was waving a Tupperware box at me.

'You hungry? I've made you some lunch. It's risotto.'

Too cold to speak, I nodded. Zoe opened the door and gestured for me to sit inside. The heat of her car was almost too much. I felt my bones, ligaments and muscles thawing, and the flesh around my shins and thighs tingled as the hot air steamed the damp in my clothes. I immediately began to dread the moment when I'd next have to step into the cold again.

'Here, take this,' said Zoe. She was shoving napkins and plastic cutlery at me. The smell and warmth of a piping hot meal was heavenly.

For the next ten minutes, I shovelled the delicious rice into my mouth and experienced a rush of returning energy. A fresh, oven-baked flatbread was passed over and my body glowed from the inside. Even the freeze around my lungs began to thaw. Zoe explained how she and her family were originally from Bournemouth and had moved to Skye to open an Airbnb. 'It's not too far away,' she said, filling my pockets with snacks and passing a Thermos cup filled with steaming coffee. 'You're more than welcome to stay with us tonight.'

I thanked her for the offer and explained how I'd just accepted another room from a family nearby. They were expecting me soon. But, bloody hell, I was tempted. Zoe's risotto was incredible and my stomach was very happy. My mind, on the other hand, was suddenly reticent about leaving the cosiness of her car, especially as my feet were close to drying. Once I restarted my walk, they would be soaked through again in a few minutes.

I sighed and stared out of the window. 'I'm six months away from finishing this,' I said, 'but it feels so bloody hard. I'm tired. I'm freezing.'

'Yeah, true,' said Zoe. 'But you more than anyone should know one important thing . . .'

'What's that?'

'That humans can do hard things.'

I was immediately lifted. *Humans can do hard things.* Just that one sentence had boosted me and when Zoe later waved me off with another beep, my inner pilot light had been reignited. I yomped through the snow again.

Still feeling nervous about the conditions, I kept up my quick pace. Having returned to the mainland via Mallaig the next day, I immediately headed for Fort William, the West Highland Way's official starting point. On the way, I passed the fantastical-looking Glenfinnan Viaduct – a series of brick arches on the West Highland Line and a landmark made famous by the Harry Potter movies. Its Hollywood stardust had been amplified with an extra sprinkling of sugar-white powder.

At that point, I'd decided to handrail the main roads, a tactical decision I believed would keep me relatively safe because I was less likely to get lost or fall into a deep snowdrift in the higher ground. Also, the risks usually associated with passing cars – as they slid and skidded across the ice and snow – weren't in play. Very few people were reckless enough to be outdoors in such horrendous conditions, let alone drive.

I was all alone.

* * *

I stayed the night in a Fort William hotel despite it being closed for winter, after the owners offered to open a single room just for me. The stay was a lifesaver, but in the morning, I was advised to stay for another night by the hotel manager. Walking The Path was too dangerous, he said sternly. And when I insisted on pressing ahead regardless, he flashed me a concerned look. I honestly couldn't blame the bloke. My younger, military-drilled self would have been furious with the older, risk-taking me. Every part of my training reminded me that what I was about to do was undeniably sketchy and I hated the thought that, at some point, I might require the mountain rescue services to save me, if something were to go wrong on the West Highland Way's remote and challenging inclines. But I also had a hell of a lot of faith in myself. I filled up my flask with hot water and checked the batteries in my headtorch. Then I cracked on.

(Important public service announcement: Do not try this out yourself. I now know that my actions were potentially life-threatening. I'd hate for anyone to put themselves at risk by following in my footsteps. The West Highland Way is *not* to be attempted during the depths of winter.)

With hindsight, I might have become a little thrown off by the doomy advice because having walked into Fort William's town centre, I then delayed the inevitable for as long as possible by sitting in a coffee shop and staring at the first steps of the West Highland Way through the window for an hour. Everything was shrouded in a thick snowy blanket. The deep purples, greens and browns of the landscape I knew from my last walk here had been replaced with glittery white mountain tops, shadowy grey valleys, and cracks and crevasses that twinkled in a bright shade of aquamarine blue. At least the weather was improving, though. The blizzards of the past few days had stopped and a bright sun now blazed overhead. On any other morning I'd have felt excited about the picture-postcard scenery around me, but knowing I would soon have to push my way through knee-high drifts in sub-zero temperatures, I flinched, procrastinated and ordered a second cup of coffee. Another hour passed. Watching the customers come and go – shivering as they stepped inside, wrapping themselves up in woolly layers as they departed – made me reconsider my plans for the day. I even thought about rebooking the hotel room. *It had been so warm.* When I then wondered about a third coffee, I knew I was fast becoming my own worst enemy.

The time had come.

Let's get this done, I told myself.

Then I stepped into the freeze.

Within ten minutes, another snowstorm had blown in and a police car pulled alongside to me to check on my physical and mental wellbeing. When I told the driver my story, he grimaced. Then he delivered a warning, just as the hotel manager had that morning.

'What you're doing, it's dangerous.'

I nodded, shivering by the roadside. It had only taken a minute for my body temperature to plummet. 'I've walked this far,' I said. 'I'll be OK'

'Well, fine. Stay on the side of the road. And be safe.'

As the car pulled away, I scanned my body from top to bottom. The freeze was gnawing on my bones. It had crystallised the moisture in my woolly hat and I could feel a skullache coming on. Meanwhile, my teeth chattered uncontrollably, causing my jaw to throb with an almost electric shock pain.

I was totally and utterly miserable. And I hadn't yet started the hardest part of my mission.

I found the trail among the powdery white carpet and pushed ahead. The mountains around me were eerily quiet and there wasn't a living thing to be seen on the horizon – no stags, no eagles and definitely no hikers in dayglo Gore-Tex. I was incredibly isolated and, unable to see the road clearly in the snow, I used the curvature of the landscape as a directional aid, prompting beeps from the odd passing car. I must have looked like a total freak show, though at least there was some good news on the accommodation front: a series of offers were arriving on social media and beds would soon be arranged for every night of my planned schedule – in hotels, Airbnbs and guest houses.

Despite this psychological respite, I was moving slowly. My legs became weighed down in the growing drifts, and my muscles were wet and heavy, like bags of soggy cement.

The temperature had swooped to a dangerous -14C and there was a very real risk of getting frostbite. When I entered Glencoe on my second day, a Hilux Jeep pulled over and the driver, a bloke with a thick beard, shouted out. He was flapping his arms animatedly, but I was so cold and tired it was impossible to understand exactly what was being said. My facial hair had frosted over, and my cheeks were bright pink and aching. To stop my eyelids from gluing together, I'd perfected the technique of blinking quickly and regularly.

I managed to refocus and leaned into the car. The driver, who was called Dom, shook his head in disbelief. 'What the hell are you doing, mate? You'll die out here.' I noticed he had an English accent.

'I know, it's mad,' I said. 'But I'm walking around Britain. I've been doing it for three years—'

'I know,' said Dom. 'I've been tracking you on Instagram. That's why I knew where to find you. But this? It's a bit extreme . . .'

I told him about my situation, the charities, how I needed to finish The Path in a year. 'It might not look like it, but I've got this,' I said. With hindsight, this was probably an attempt to convince myself, rather than the person staring at me in disbelief.

Dom laughed. 'Look, I can drive you all the way to Glasgow if you like. It might save you from pneumonia.'

I thanked him and told him I was determined to push on. There was a hotel waiting for me in Tyndrum and I could rest for two nights and dry my clothes. *I'm going to be OK.* But if I stopped now, I wouldn't reach it in time.

Dom nodded, not looking entirely persuaded. 'Well, if you

say so, pal. I can't force you to come with me.' Then he drove off, waving from his window as he disappeared into the white.

That night, as I rested in the hotel, I fantasised about taking up Dom's offer. Even though Glasgow was only four or five days away, it would require a miracle to get there, and according to a series of anxious texts from friends, my location was set to be the coldest point in the UK the next day, with temperatures dropping to as low as -16C. I felt sick. I'd reached my lowest point on The Path and was emotionally and physically exhausted. The cold had drained my internal battery, in much the same way that it had drained my phone.

The following morning, as my trudge resumed, I fell into a disorientating emotional spiral. At one point, I even debated the merits of sleeping in a nearby clump of trees, just so I could rest for an hour or two. *You can sit,* I thought. *Grab some sleep and recharge. You'll be back to 100 per cent afterwards.* But I was selling myself a dangerous lie. I had no sleeping bag or tent for shelter. I was dangerously drowsy. And if I closed my eyes, I'd likely never wake up again. What I was experiencing was the early phases of hypothermia and there was a very real risk I might freeze to death.

Then the miracle I so badly needed arrived.

The Hilux Jeep had returned. I saw it on the road framing the edges of the West Highland Way at the Bridge of Orchy. Beeping his horn loudly and waving to me in the distance was Dom, the motorist from yesterday.

'Hey! Warrior Walker!' he shouted from the window, having pulled over nearby. 'Get in here, pal.'

This time, I couldn't find an excuse to say no. I dusted away the snow from my clothes and bundled in alongside him, feeling the comforting blast of hot air from the car's dashboard vents.

'I couldn't stop thinking about what you were doing,' said Dom.

I laughed wryly. 'Oh yeah?'

'Yeah! I mean, it's so risky. And it's so inspiring. Just deciding to walk around Britain because you could. In these conditions. Lots of people would want to do that, but they can't.'

I murmured a vague response. Fatigue was sweeping in like an avalanche and I could barely keep my eyes open. Dom reached into the back of the car for a rucksack. It was obvious I was struggling.

'Anyway, me and my wife were talking about you last night,' he said, rummaging through the bag. 'And she made you a cake. And I've made you some coffee.'

I mumbled a thank you. I felt so grateful for his arrival but articulating an appropriate response seemed impossible. Instead, I shovelled the cake into my mouth and sipped the piping hot drink. 'I'm so fucked,' I said, doing my best to smile. 'So fucking fucked.'

'Well, look. You can just sit here with me for a couple of hours,' said Dom. 'I've got nowhere to be, so keep warm for as long as you want.'

I thanked him again and closed my eyes. All I wanted to do was sleep.

The Path could wait for a bit.

* * *

The rest of the walk to Milngavie, the West Highland Way's

end point this time around, was every bit as painful as the first two days. The snow turned to slush and I slipped and crashed along the trail, past fences and route markers that were now, mercifully, making themselves known in the thaw. Trying to keep my spirits up, I stared at the bright blue skies around me and thought of seeing Alice again. I couldn't wait to kiss her.

I had some company as I finished the West Highland Way. Mitch Hutchcraft, the former Marine now famous for running, cycling and swimming over 12,800 kilometres in a 2025 journey that included the summit of Mount Everest, joined me for 24 hours. It felt good to be walking this stretch with someone, having spent so much time wandering alone with nothing but the crunch of my boots in the snow for company. Mitch's incredible adventure was very much in the development stages at that point and we chatted enthusiastically about his plans. I was excited for him. Our conversation was the perfect distraction from the pain in my back, legs and feet.

When I eventually stepped out of the mountains and valleys of Inverarnan and Rowardennan, past Loch Lomond and through Dryman and Milngavie, the experience became a mirror image of my previous transit through the West Highland Way, though rather than stepping into a Narnia-like landscape, I was now leaving and returning to the humdrum of everyday life. Suddenly dropped into an urban landscape on the edges of Glasgow, I felt underwhelmed by the towny architecture. There were traffic lights and roundabouts; road diversion signs and bus stops; gloomy tower blocks and industrial buildings. Part of me wanted to circumnavigate Glasgow for a more scenic route.

I was also fearful of what might await me in the city centre. The last time I was in Glasgow, my chest had tightened and my lungs had clenched in a terrifying panic attack. I reassured myself with a reminder that I was so very different to the person that had freaked out in a crowded coffee shop – leaner and fitter, emotionally stronger and brimming with self-confidence. But I was equally excited for my next challenge, the English border, because beyond that was Wales and the South West Coast Path, the Hampshire, Sussex and Kent seaside, and London's magnetising end point. The route towards these trails was arduous, a sidewinding path that would first take me into the Lake District again before following the northwest's jagged coastline as it moved to and from the Irish Sea. But I was ready for it. There was belief.

After the West Highland Way, I could do just about anything.

CHAPTER TWENTY-FOUR

YOU'LL NEVER WALK ALONE

I left Glasgow and moved through Ayrshire, where I stayed in a high turreted castle on the Craufurdland Estate, which was apparently frequented by the Royals during their holidays. Its walls and libraries were lined with antique books and, in a safe, was a framed letter from Mary, Queen of Scots. I then crossed the Scottish border in February and headed towards Carlisle and Keswick for a second walk into the Lake District. I was unstoppable. After battling through the West Highland Way's energy-sapping snowdrifts in dangerous temperatures, the tarmac paths and marked trails leading me south acted like a travelator. I only had to pull on my boots to surge forward.

At times, my overenthusiasm got the better of me. Whenever the pace increased too quickly or aggressively, my feet became bruised and swollen, and my knees and ankles throbbed and cracked for hours. But I was feeling strong and able to maintain a steady rhythm. This was encouraging news; I had good reason to tick off the kilometres in the north of England because I'd been presented with an exciting incentive. While walking with Mitch on the West Highland Way several weeks earlier, my phone had pinged with an Instagram notification. I was now being followed by Bruce Grobbelaar, the former Liverpool goalkeeper and footballing legend.

What? I thought, disbelievingly.

Excitedly, I showed Mitch the phone. He was a Liverpool fan. *Surely it can't actually be him?*

Mitch stared at the profile. 'It seems legit, mate,' he said, eventually.

I had then scrolled through Bruce's page. The photos looked genuine. His profile described him as a goalkeeper, coach, manager, public speaker, golfer, and a guest supporter of Sparks and Golden 5 (which I assumed were charities) plus one or two adverts for his upcoming personal appearances. If this wasn't the real Bruce Grobbelaar, the account holder was doing a bloody good impression. I'd messaged him instantly, hoping for the best, but ready to block the account if I picked up on any weird vibes. Bruce had responded straight away. Apparently, he was travelling, a claim backed up by his posts, but he wanted to talk about my journey face to face. Would I like to be his guest at Liverpool FC for a Premier League game in the next couple of months? I'd tingled with excitement at the suggestion. Though I was a Manchester United supporter – sworn rivals to Liverpool – I was also a football fan. Watching a match as the guest of a former title-winning icon was too good an opportunity to pass up. I checked the fixture list. Liverpool were playing newly promoted Luton Town on 21 February at Anfield, their home ground. So I pushed my body to get there.

In one or two exchanges, Bruce had made it clear that he didn't think I'd make it in time for the match, so I did everything to prove him wrong. I eventually reached Liverpool with a day to spare. And when he welcomed me into his hotel suite, introducing me to family and friends, I felt like an awkward teenager. I couldn't quite believe I was meeting the same person I'd once watched on *Match of the Day* as a kid. Bruce then peppered me with questions about life, the walk and what I'd seen, before explaining I would be watching the game in a box later that night. There would be free drinks and food; I'd likely be surrounded by famous ex-players and club ambassadors, among them Phil Neal and Terry McDermott. I seemed to have stepped into a parallel universe. And when a fan came over and asked me to take a photograph of him with his favourite Liverpool player, Bruce politely corrected him.

'Nobody asks the Warrior Walker to do the pictures,' he said, laughing, before taking the shot himself.

The poor fan looked at me, bemused as to why the scruffy bloke with wild hair and a scraggly beard should be the centre of attention in a room commanded by one of the most famous Liverpool players of all time. I smiled sheepishly, wanting to tell him that I felt exactly the same way.

* * *

A series of happy reunions took place when I crossed the Welsh border. As promised, Louis, Joey and Ant met me on The Path, which felt especially poignant. Louis had stuck to his promise of walking with me in every country on my journey and his commitment was impressive. The meeting was also bittersweet: I couldn't hang around to chat and the haste with which I was moving from person to person felt painfully rushed. Speed had become my priority. The catching up with mates would have to wait.

This was so very different to the first lap, when I'd connected with people as complete strangers and departed their homes as close friends. I'd had time to spare back then and no schedule to stick to. But to complete the Victory Lap in my stated target of one year, I needed to arrive in London by early June. It was March already; the first bursts of spring were dappling the grass and trees along the path, and the morning light was growing soft and hazy. I noticed blooming flowers and new shoots along the trail, and every flash of colour was a sign that the clock was ticking. Staying for more than a night in one place was now an unaffordable luxury.

There was one exception: Sandy and her husband Ian, a couple in their sixties, who lived in Aberdovey. They had kindly sheltered me in 2022 when a succession of life-threatening storms whipped in off the Irish Sea. The weather warnings at the time had been stark. No one was to leave the house unless it was absolutely necessary. And as the three of us had hunkered down, the rain and wind drumming at the windows and rattling the roof tiles, we shared stories and picked apart the mysteries of life, love and the universe. Sandy and Ian, like so many people on that first lap, soon came to feel like close family and I remembered not wanting the storms to blow out. I hadn't wanted to leave. Fast forward a few years, and they were also evidence that life on The Path was unrelenting. In the time since I'd last seen them, Sandy had been diagnosed with cancer, undergone treatment and was now in remission.

The experience hadn't diminished her. If people could be divided into the two categories of drains or radiators, then Sandy was a furnace. When she arrived to pick me up, it was as if nothing had changed. Her diminutive, pixie-ish frame bristled with excitement and, as we drove to her home – a warm, loving house that sat on a cliff edge – I explained how my world had changed too.

'There's a new person in my life, Sandy,' I said.

Suddenly, my pocket vibrated. When I looked at my phone, I laughed. 'Talk of the devil. It's her. It's Alice.'

Then I stressed. Alice had recently stated that she would only ever call me on The Path if there was an emergency because she didn't want to distract me. So, this couldn't be good.

'Alice? You OK?'

There was silence at the other end.

'Alice?'

Then I heard a sniffle. She was crying. *Shit.*

'Oh my god . . . what's up?'

Alice tried to explain but nothing was coming out. She was struggling to breathe.

'I'm not in a good place right now,' she sobbed eventually. 'Everything's falling apart . . .'

Alice finally explained how her boss had suggested that she take some time off. She'd noticed she was struggling with the workload. Now Alice was figuring out what to do. 'She told me: "Wherever Paul is, *find him.*"'

Sandy looked across at me in the car. She could hear pretty much everything.

'Tell her to come here tomorrow,' she said.

I couldn't believe it. Silently, I mouthed back at her: *Is that OK?*

Sandy was nodding. 'Yes. Tell her she's welcome. And Paul?' *Yes?*

'Go and get her. Don't let her come here alone.' She reached across and grabbed my arm reassuringly.

I nodded, relaying the plan to Alice, who sobbed her thanks and started to pack her bags.

The following afternoon, we were both back in Sandy's kitchen, as Alice explained what had happened over the past few weeks. The winter and the long dark nights had got to her and she'd felt alone without me. The fact that I was so far away, and uncertain on when I'd next be with her in Bristol, had become too painful. When work then became a massive struggle, her life looked to be spiralling out of control. I cuddled her tightly as Sandy explained that we were welcome to stay at the house for as long as we liked. 'Use it as another base camp,' she said before explaining that to keep me on track, she would act as my support car, ferrying me to and from my updated position on the map every morning and evening. I could clock up the miles as Alice rested in the warm and dry.

But Alice wasn't having any of it. 'I want to come with you.'

I glowed inside. I loved the idea. 'Are you sure?'

'Yeah, I want to fully experience what this is all about.'

The following morning, we walked all day, Alice wrapped up in her warm winter gear as we pushed on through a succession of spring showers. At times, the rain seemed to smash into us at right angles. Then the wind threatened to blow us from the trail and into the churning tide and rocks below. But we held fast, talking for ages, breathing in the sea air and feeling the therapeutic shock of nature at its unpredictable worst. Even when we were soaked through, being outdoors was a tonic for the soul.

'I can see why you love this so much,' she said one night over dinner.

I smiled. 'Oh yeah? Why's that?' It felt validating to hear her say it.

'Because you get to see how kind people are,' she continued. 'Like Sandy. And when you tell them what you're doing, they change physically. It's like they lift up. But also, I can see how hard this is. *It's relentless.* There's no hiding from the weather, or the aching, or the heavy backpack. I don't know how you've been doing it all this time.'

On the fifth day of walking the Welsh coastline, with nearly 55 kilometres in our legs, Alice insisted on carrying my day bag. I protested. 'You don't have to do that.'

She grabbed at the straps. 'No. But I want to. I'm a strong, independent woman. Let me feel the weight for a bit.'

Everything had come full circle. Around six months previously, Alice had reached out to me online, having been inspired by my healing mission. When a dark moment of her own had arrived, she'd come to The Path as a way of reaching a similar level of peace.

'I'm in the right place,' she said, having walked ahead steadily, her body adjusting to the weight across her shoulders.

And so was I.

* * *

For the first time in my life, I was fully comfortable with my true self: *a person on The Path* – and the idea was both physical and metaphorical. I was also cementing some of the ideas I'd first mentioned to people a couple of years previously: *that I was walking towards my own death*. I spoke more openly about it, without fear or judgement, though I still received a funny look every now and then, probably because the concept sounded so bloody morbid. Yeah, there was a fatalistic totality to it, but the deeper meaning of what I'd been feeling was cut through with optimism.

Four years ago, stuck at home with Dad, in a dead-end job, grieving the end of an important relationship, I'd sensed my end approaching. At one point, I'd wanted to gain some control over my miserable circumstances by speeding up the process, and that feeling, plus the fact I'd been able to turn away from it by connecting with people and places, had given me a new perspective. Death was coming for us all. No one gets out of their story alive. It was down to all of us to write the best narratives possible for ourselves, so that's what I was doing.

I'd also realised that very few people acknowledge their limited time. They live as if there are an infinite number of perfect days ahead and take the good things for granted. Don't get me wrong – I didn't want to die. But to truly live, I had to recognise mortality's presence and squeeze every drop of life from my current moment. The ground under my feet. The sun on my face. The leaves flickering in the wind. Whenever people asked me for my inspiration, I told them honestly. *Memento mori*: remember you will die. The concept was my new North Star and because of it, I vowed to love people for longer, squeeze friends tighter, and to enjoy every day while I was happy and healthy. Whenever I said hello to a stranger or sipped on the first coffee of the morning, I treated the experience like it was my last, knowing it would very much be the case at some point in the future.

This belief was drawing more and more similarly minded people into my orbit, individuals who shared the same ideals. They either already lived in the moment or were approaching that same mindset for one reason or another. Often it was because they'd been close to death themselves. Others had experienced a bereavement in the family or were dealing with some terrible trauma. And I met them everywhere.

Less than a week after Alice had left The Path, I stepped through St Dogmaels near Cardigan. The village was beautiful. Set in a small valley and sliced open by an estuary, it was bookended by a crumbling abbey on one side and a bank of rich green fields on the other. It was the sort of place you'd see drawn on a biscuit tin in the 1980s. I wandered through a quiet street, past the chippy. And then I heard someone shouting my name in the distance. At first, I thought I was imagining things. I hadn't met anyone from St Dogmaels during the first lap and I certainly didn't have any friends nearby. But when I turned and looked, I saw a woman racing towards me. She must have been in her sixties, but she was pretty quick on her feet and waving excitedly.

'Paul!' she yelled again. 'The Warrior Walker!'

The woman got closer. I saw that her face was kind. She certainly didn't seem annoyed, angry or upset, which was good news. Her hair was very short, grey and swept back. Her eyes seemed to sparkle. There was a friendly aura. But I still had no idea who she was.

'Hi . . . Yeah, I'm Paul. Have we met?'

'No, we haven't . . . I'm Sue,' she said, squeezing my hand. She was breathing hard. The run had knocked the stuffing from her.

'My friend told me about you,' she said at last. 'She met you a couple of days ago and she told me what you're all about. *The Warrior Walker this, the Warrior Walker that.* I'm so glad I saw you walk past.'

Sue pointed a thumb back to her doorstep. 'Fancy a cuppa?'

Well, yeah. 'Why not?' I said, knowing I was almost done for the day.

Sue then showed me into her home, introduced me to her husband, Pete, and made up a plate of ham and pickle sandwiches, a pot of tea and a second plate stacked with shortbread biscuits. Because of the thousands of calories I was burning, I was always hungry, and as I wolfed down the first round of sarnies, Sue readied another. All the while she bombarded me with questions. Her mood was so inquisitive and warm-hearted that I poured everything out to her in the long version – no shortcuts or fast-forwarding. Then Sue looked down at her hands. It seemed like she was about to cry.

'Simon would have loved you,' she said, trying to smile but failing. Sue's lips were trembling. Her eyes were teary.

Who's Simon . . . ? I wondered, thinking back to Jane and our emotional meeting outside Northumberland.

'My son,' said Sue. 'A real adventurer. Always full of stories about "randoms" – his *word* – people he'd meet travelling. He loved walking around in his shorts with a pair of sandals and white socks. That might have looked weird on some people, but he seemed to pull it off . . .'

Pete leaned towards us in his armchair. 'Strong legs, that one,' he said, proudly.

But Sue was really crying now. I put my arm around her as Pete reached for a box of tissues. 'Sue . . . What's wrong?' I said.

'He got a job in Amsterdam. And he was always complaining of headaches, but nothing too serious. Then one day we got a call to say that he'd died. A brain haemorrhage.'

'There you go, love,' said Pete. He was waving a hankie under her nose. 'Try not to get too upset.'

I felt my heart breaking and squeezed Sue tight.

'He was barely 30,' she said, blowing her nose loudly. 'When I saw a picture of you online, walking around with a backpack on, curly hair, shorts, socks . . . You reminded me of him. You have the same spirit.'

We talked for an hour or so, with Sue sharing stories about Simon and bringing out the photos; me reliving the places where we both might have travelled or crossed paths. By the time I left her front door, we were two friends with a strong bond. I felt as if I knew Simon. I certainly knew Sue and Pete. The afternoon had been healing for all of us.

By the time I'd crossed the English border in April, all 1,400 odd kilometres of the Wales Coast Path had been walked in

28 days. Suddenly, the thought of reaching The Path's end was losing appeal again, as it had done on the first lap, though there was no way I could imagine a third go-around. Instead, I'd come to the conclusion that the finish line wasn't important, it was the living along the way: the conversations with 'randoms', the strangers who turned into friends and the warmth of healing, especially when that healing was done with others. I'd realised that too many people in the real world were overly focused on money and materialism. They fretted about property prices, stock portfolios and the politics of greed. And their fears of missing out on something they believed was owed to them had led them down a dark path. They were fuelled by rage, division and prejudice; their language came from a place of anger rather than love. But on The Path, with next to nothing in the way of cash or *stuff*, I felt like the richest person in the UK. That's because I was meeting with beautiful people like Sandy and Sue, and enjoying the ride rather than wondering what was happening back at the start line or searching for the first hint of an end point. My priority was the everything in between. Living in the moment had created a sense that everything was at peace.

That was the magic of The Path.

CHAPTER TWENTY-FIVE

A STILLNESS

Though I was familiar with the South West Coast Path's disorientating tracks and undulating terrain, the route was still fraught with psychological hurdles, such as the daunting inclines of The Rollercoaster, or the never-ending trail ahead that seemed to sidewind around the Cornish cliffs like the world's longest boa constrictor. Luckily, the weather was behaving in a relatively benign fashion. The blistering summer heat had yet to kick in, and I was able to move quickly and steadily during the lengthening evenings, cranking through 40-, 50- and 60-kilometre days without too much stress. After four years walking the British coastline, I'd become even more attuned to the nuances of physical challenge, with all its second winds and muscular surprises, and keenly alert to my body's rhythms. Once I'd passed Start Point in Devon – a prominent headland – I felt like the home stretch had arrived and I was bloody happy to be there.

This overwhelming sense of gratitude peaked when I approached Lulworth Cove, the scene of my very first night as a Warrior Walker in 2020. I could clearly remember bedding down into that foxhole to sleep, the moon spotlighting a deep blue stretch of water ahead, the tide washing softly across the rocks below. Before the arrival of the stag, I'd been unaware of the risks around me on The Path – some of them imagined, some of them very real. Nearly four years later, that same shallow indentation in the grass was still visible and I sat down in it for a few moments. Most walkers would likely pass this spot in the landscape without thinking, but to me, it was a symbolic landmark that represented a huge moment of change. Immediately, every hope and fear from that first evening charged at me: my life had been terrifying back then; I was uncertain of the future and wanting to turn around while knowing that I couldn't. I patted the grass gently, hoping to connect with my old self somehow, the emotion catching in my throat. I understood that this little spot marked the opening steps in a four-year journey of millions. It was the first page in my new story.

The moment was strangely jarring. I didn't recognise the lead character from the narrative because I was undeniably altered now. Equally, the depressed, desperate and near-suicidal me from before couldn't have possibly imagined the protagonist sat in that same scooped-out divot four years later – the person I was to become. The events ahead would have felt too fantastical, almost unbelievable, but I had achieved them. And my life was so much better as a result. I had also reached an understanding of the moments that had led me to a very bad place and was now educated in where to go if my darkest emotions ever returned. To humans – *because they were beautiful*. To nature – *because it was a power up for my soul*. And to physical exercise – *because it was a tonic for all my stresses*. On The Path, I'd experienced just about every emotion, positive and negative, and at first, all of them had overwhelmed me. I then thought back to Zoe and her pep talk during that frozen day on Skye. Fuck me, she'd been right. *Humans can do hard things*. I was living proof of it.

As before, it would take other people to drive the point home. After all, it was one thing *believing* that I'd turned some psychological corner or cracked an existential puzzle. But the *knowing* only happened when, yet again, friends and family reflected those same self-beliefs back at me. When I'd passed through Cornwall and returned to the Hidden Hut beach restaurant, mates remarked on how much more in control I seemed. Apparently, I was now more assertive and focused. Later, in Bournemouth, I met up with Tommy, my old training partner from those dreary, depressing months that led into the first lockdown, and, after that, my stepbrother, Tom, who joined me for a few hours, dressed in his suit and a pair of smart shoes. The comments from both were incredibly validating. *You look great,* they said. *You seem happier. You're more self-assured than before.* For the first time ever, I was able to acknowledge the compliments as being genuine because, deep down, I was happy with my truest self.

The changes weren't just personal, though. The connection to my environment had altered too and as I wandered past Bournemouth, my hometown for so long, any remaining emotional links seemed to have been cut loose – I felt indifferent and disinterested. Partly, this was down to acceptance. I didn't really have any special memories of Bournemouth. I was born there and it had pretty much held me prisoner because as a younger person, I'd believed there was a certain duty in sticking around and making things work, even when they were broken beyond repair. And while Dad still lived nearby, I was understanding of the fact that he wouldn't be coming to meet me at any point – and that was fine. I was at peace with our relationship and all its complications. Similarly, I knew there was pride to be taken in moving on and starting over again, especially when there was a long list of places around the UK that could potentially become home. If Alice was with me, I'd be fine.

Meanwhile, more people beyond my immediate friendship circle were taking an interest in the Victory Lap. As I moved closer to the finish line, there was an exponential spurt in Instagram followers – among them, a series of journalists who wanted to profile me. I'd already been interviewed by several local newspapers as I'd passed through their constituencies, but now the big guns were out. Waiting in my DMs were requests from local TV stations and lifestyle websites. The BBC and ITV wanted to talk after I'd finished. And when I reached Southampton, a taxi transported me to Meridian TV, where I conducted a studio interview in my still-sweaty kit. At Brighton, I appeared on a local radio station. All of this was great fun, but my profile eventually went up a level when Sky News called. They wanted to speak to me in their London studio, which was close to the Houses of Parliament. At the time, I was still on the south coast, and when the producer asked for my estimated time of arrival at the finish line, I checked the map.

'I'll be there on 20 June,' I said, confidently.

The voice on the other end snorted. 'No way! That's only a few days away.'

The sense of disbelief made me laugh, though it was disappointing, even as I'd become used to it. From the moment I'd set off on the first lap, a series of doubters had knocked my potential. Now, with the walk so close to completion, a weird sense of pessimism – always from outsiders; always beyond my control – still clung to my ambitions, despite the achievements. Given that I enjoyed being the underdog, I bit my tongue and confirmed an appearance in their studio on my stated date.

'I'll be there, no problem,' I said confidently. I didn't need to point out the stats and my progress so far.

To keep myself focused, I picked out my last clean t-shirt, a white number from Primark, and pushed it to the bottom of the bag. I wanted something clean to wear for my big TV moment.

* * *

Then it arrived, finally: the breaking point.

As I arced around the south coast, past East Sussex before turning north around Kent, my body rebelled one last time. It even hurt to take my shoes off, I was in that bad a state. Going smooth and fast on the South West Coast Path, while comfortable in the moment, had battered me, but I wasn't altogether surprised. Over the past four years, I'd walked thousands and thousands of kilometres and if my body were a car, I'd have been well in need of a thorough service. But I also wondered whether I was experiencing an emotional reaction to a fast-approaching end point – a bit like when somebody really needs a pee on the walk home and when they finally reach their front door, the urgency intensifies. Rather than grumbling, I clenched my fists and stepped into a psychological fight with my own body. The finish line was only days away.

One of the good things about having a military background was that I'd been well drilled in shutting out most forms of physical discomfort. During training manoeuvres, it was drummed into us that if we didn't reach a certain rendezvous point by a certain time, it would likely result in us being killed in a situation where the bombs and bullets were flying around for real. The helicopters would leave without us. The cavalry would depart. And we would be stranded. That emotional context was an incredibly powerful motivator and on exercises, dozens of Royal Marines Commandos moved as one to their destination, not wanting to suffer the imagined consequences.

I also had a very strong sense of visualisation: emotionally, I could take myself to places and situations without too much bother. So I pictured the repercussions of quitting so close to the end in a distressing doom loop. The Sky News interview might fall through. My charity work would have been for nothing. I'd let Alice down. *The helicopter would leave.* I played the game for hours but the effort was gruelling. Weeks previously, when on the South West Coast Path, I'd often walk for 50 kilometres without really stopping. Now I was pausing twice a kilometre. The limit of my ability, a barrier I'd hoped to reach eventually, was now closing in. I could sense it in my peripheral and it was brutalising me.

Friends came out of nowhere to help, inspired into action by one or two pained posts on social media. As I moved around Margate, everything seemed to be on the attack. There was no shelter and it was a boiling hot June day. At times, it felt as if the concrete was on fire and every footstep was agonising. I couldn't even listen to music because the sound in my ears was so excruciating. When I looked down at my phone, there was an overwhelming sense of frustration. I was so close to the end but I still had 36 hours of walking to go.

Joey once again arrived to support me when I most needed it, joining The Path as I trudged under a bright, clear moon. It seemed to shine a line for me as I staggered until 3am, looking to the gods and the stars, hoping for some respite from the hurt. Joey had a place in Kent. And when I later crashed at his place, I power napped for 30 minutes, before he stirred me with a plate of toasted bagels and peanut butter. I washed it down with a protein shake. I felt like a marathon runner on his last legs.

The following *final* morning, as I trailed the Thames Estuary into London, I met Alastair Humphreys, an explorer famous for both biking 74,000 kilometres around the world in over four years and for completing the notorious Marathon des Sables – a 240km race across the Sahara – with a broken foot in 2008. His book sat on Alice's shelf and when he'd contacted me, I jumped at the chance of meeting him in a coffee shop along the route, even though I could barely talk or stand. In the delirium of finishing, I have no real idea of where we went for our conversation, but I do remember that Al wanted me to slow down. He'd recognised that I might have been close to doing some serious damage to myself and wanted me to proceed with caution. All of which was ironic, given his experience in the Sahara, but I appreciated the sentiment.

I wasn't going to listen though; my mind was set. 'I gotta go,' I said, over and over. 'I'm doing what I said I would do.'

Finally, as I moved closer to London, Paul, a mate I'd previously met on the trail in Gosport, called out of the blue.

'I'm right behind you on the road,' he said. 'I've driven down, I'll help you to finish.'

Paul was living in London at the time and had been nearby. But I didn't need the help. I wanted solitude because I didn't have the emotional bandwidth for conversation, no matter how big or small.

Fucking hell, I thought. *I really don't fancy this.*

When Paul finally caught up with me that afternoon, I was in a terrible mood. He was excited and wanted to talk and make videos, but I didn't have the strength for any of it. It soon showed.

'Paul, I'm not being horrible, but I can't chat,' I said eventually. 'Alice is going to call me at some point and I'm waiting for that. I'm saving my energy for her. That's it.'

Sometimes it takes an outsider to realise that we're in trouble, especially when we've become blinded to a problem through fatigue, emotion or stress. Mine was that I seemed to be on the verge of snapping as I moved deeper into London, passing through the suburbs and then onto a stretch along the Thames where some of the more famous landmarks were coming into view. I passed the Thames Barrier and the Cutty Sark in Greenwich. As I pressed on, it was possible to see St Paul's Cathedral in the distance. But I could barely carry my bag, so

Paul stuck around and helped me with the load. My hands had clenched into boxer's fists and spasmed painfully. My back, neck and shoulders burned with lactic acid. Eventually, I turned to him and grimaced.

'I'm struggling here, mate,' I said, finally admitting to my pain.

He smiled knowingly. 'It's OK, bro,' he said. 'You can do this. The last stretch was always going to be the hardest.'

My anger seemed to melt away in the heat. An hour or so previously, I'd hated the thought of him being there. I'd been so locked into the battle of *Me Versus Me* that I'd lost sight of what was important – the people and the places. At one point, I'd even hidden my phone away because I didn't want to speak to anyone. Now, with Paul alongside me, acting as a motivational speaker, it felt as if everything was going to be OK.

'I'm sorry about earlier,' I said sadly. 'I'm happy you're here.'

'It's cool, mate.'

'I know. I just needed to say it. I was hoping nobody else would be here but me.'

Paul stopped. 'What do you mean?'

I leaned against a railing, barely able to stand. 'I think on the first lap, I wanted to know who I was,' I said. 'But also, I wanted people to be impressed. Like, external validation. On this lap, I know who I am and I'm happy with myself. I don't need anyone else. So, this isn't for anyone else. It's me proving something to me.'

Paul gave me a hug. 'I get it, mate,' he said, pointing down the street.

The finish line was in sight.

When I eventually arrived in central London a few painful hours later, the walking stopped. I sat in a pub, ordered a pint of lager and called Alice.

Then I told her I loved her and cried.

The magic of The Path smothered me. For so long, I'd clung to the fact that I was doing something special. And having been swallowed up by London's spires and skyscrapers, I realised: I'd *done* something special. The little boy in me was excited again. I thought about Nan and Grandad and our time on Skye. Then I remembered the buried locket at Calanais and felt proud, knowing I'd found some closure in a period of hopelessness. But I was also of a mind that everything that had happened, and *was* happening, had been backed by a powerful sense of purpose. Had I not set off on my walk around Britain in 2020 who knows what would have happened to me. If I hadn't repeated the effort on the Victory Lap, there's no way I'd have met Alice. These discoveries meant that The Path was now a constant, a fixed point of safety in my life, and no matter where I was in the world, no matter what I was doing, or the state of the weather, I could return to it at any time by simply pulling on my shoes and stepping outside. I could walk for ten minutes or ten years. The magic of The Path wasn't going to let me down. Simply knowing it existed was my new superpower.

I finished my pint. My skin shivered with goosebumps. For the first time in four years, I was happy to sit still and do nothing. I only had to breathe.

I had found my enough.

ACKNOWLEDGEMENTS

This book for me is so much more than words on a page.

I have so many people to thank, too many actually, so here goes.

Thank you to all those who have helped me not just on this walk but in life.

Thank you to every single person who helped me in some form when I walked for four years. Without your kindness, love and support it would have taken me much longer.

Thank you to all the 'radiators' who have given me warmth, belief, kindness, support and always ensured the fire within me remains burning, no matter what situation I find myself in.

Thank you equally to all the 'drains' who tried to – and still do try – to bring me down, doubt my integrity and challenges in life and, ultimately, don't want me succeed. You give me the energy to prove you wrong, so keep going!

Now for some name-dropping of people that don't appear in the book.

Thank you to Matt Allen as without our weekly check-ins, there would be no book. Your talent for listening to me and getting my words down in written form is a magical one, my friend.

Thank you to Rory Scarfe for the belief in me that this could even be a thing.

Thank you to Joe at Blink Publishing and Bonnier for seeing that this project was something that needed to be put out to the masses.

Thank you to all the people involved in the production of this book, no matter what your role was.

Thank you to Miles for being a great friend and someone I would always want to be my first person to call if ever I get into a situation – no matter how big or small that may be.

Thank you to Marcus, Melanie and Gabby for the epic trip to Italy, and showing me great kindness throughout.

Thank you to Rory for sending me a message that would ultimately change my life.

Thank you to Alice for all the things that just can't be put into words.

Thank you to all the people I definitely missed out.